KU-403-063

LOCAL CHURCH PLANTING

We need many more books on Church Planting, but above all books from 'hands on' practitioners. Peter Nodding has this supreme qualification. This book thoroughly meets the needs of those wanting practical church planting inspiration and knowhow. We need many more churches planting in order to evangelize 'in depth', the United Kingdom once again.

ROGER FORSTER
Ichthus Christian Fellowship, London

Peter Nodding asks hard and practical questions about Church Planting and, arising out of his personal, sometimes painful, experience, provides realistic answers. There are several books on the vision and theology of church planting. This one fills a gap in telling local churches and local communities of churches 'how'.

DEREK TIDBALL
Secretary for Mission, Baptist Union

SPRINGDALE COLLEGE
UNITY BUSINESS CENTRE
26 ROUNDHAY ROAD
LEEDS L22 5NA

SPRINGDALE COLLEGE
UNITY BUSINESS CENTRE
26 ROUNDHAY ROAD
LEEDS LS7 4HA

LOCAL
CHURCH PLANTING
──── *A practical handbook* ────

PETER NODDING

Marshall Pickering
An Imprint of HarperCollinsPublishers

Marshall Pickering is an Imprint of
HarperCollins*Religious*
Part of HarperCollins*Publishers*
77–85 Fulham Palace Road, London W6 8JB

First published in Great Britain
in 1994 by Marshall Pickering

1 3 5 7 9 10 8 6 4 2

Copyright © 1994 Peter Nodding

Peter Nodding asserts the moral right to be
identified as the author of this work

A catalogue record for this book is
available from the British Library

ISBN 0 551 02837–8

Photypeset by
Harper Phototypesetters Limited, Northampton, England
Printed and bound in Great Britain by
HarperCollinsManufacturing Glasgow

CONDITIONS OF SALE
This book is sold subject to the condition that it
shall not, by way of trade or otherwise, be lent, re-sold,
hired out or otherwise circulated without the publisher's
prior consent in any form of binding or cover other
than that in which it is published and without a
similar condition including this condition being
imposed on the subsequent purchaser.

All rights reserved. No part of this publication may be
reproduced, stored in a retrieval system, or transmitted,
in any form or by any means, electronic, mechanical,
photocopying, recording or otherwise, without the prior
permission of the publishers.

To my wife, Wendy

ACKNOWLEDGEMENTS

I would like to thank my secretary, Monica Gurtler, for typing (and re-typing) the manuscript, and Marian Westlake and Nancy Bullock (Millmead members) for checking each chapter and making helpful comments and corrections. Also, all those who filled in questionnaires and gave details of their church plant situations.

CONTENTS

FOREWORD

It was said to me recently: 'There are two types of Christian in Britain today. There are those who think that church planting is a good idea — and then there are those who are actually church planting.'

Having been involved in several church plants, I knew what this person meant. Of course church planting is a good idea. The early Church grew firstly through the addition of new members and then by the multiplication of congregations. Every new congregation is a new centre for mission and utilizes all the more effectively the gifts of God's people. The arguments that church planting is an essential ingredient to effective evangelism are, to my mind, thoroughly persuasive. Yet it needs to be said that church planting is never easy and those who attempt it soon find this out, sometimes at considerable cost. Giving birth to new life is never easy, however much joy and excitement it may involve. It is for this reason that Peter Nodding's practical and realistic book is to be welcomed, not to make it easier, but as a guide to what may be expected along the way and how it may best be turned to good.

Peter knows a thing or two about the subject, and what he knows is the product of direct experience. There are some whose ability and competence thrust them beyond others in the practice of mission. From the beginning of his ministry Peter has struck emphases which some of the rest of us are only now catching up with. After serving as a Cliff College evangelist and studying theology at St John's College, Nottingham, he began his ministry at West Bridgford, Nottingham. The church he led there became a model of what many a more church should be, spawning new congregations, helping to revitalize struggling causes further afield, sending a constant stream of people into full-time ministry.

It is largely out of that experience, transposed now to Millmead, Guildford, that this book comes. Yet it is not the type to make people quail at the enormity of the church planting task. It makes wisdom accessible to all.

We cannot help but welcome the new emphasis on growth through new congregations which has gripped new churches and historic denominations alike. It is profoundly encouraging to learn of the strategies being devised by denominational bodies and newer networks. But we do need to pass beyond the 'romantic' stage, that mood in which every church which is moving with the times needs to be able to accredit itself by talking of its church planting programme. What is needed is a strategy whereby in hard-headed, undramatic ways a myriad of small decisions to plant will be taken by churches all over, which cumulatively will amount to a large step forward. This book, with its emphasis on the local and its realistic approach, will be of enormous help to many churches in this process.

Nigel G. Wright
Spurgeon's College,
London

INTRODUCTION

God is challenging us to place evangelism at the centre of the work of the local church. This means granting it priority time in the hearts and thoughts of leaders and people. And it means a great deal more than declaring a decade of evangelism. Individual churches and Christians require a complete overhaul to put evangelism in place. I believe that we have begun to witness the beginnings of this vital readjustment.

This book is committed to the principle of geographical or neighbourhood evangelism. This means getting alongside people and earning the right to share the Gospel where we live. It means becoming aware of the people who live in the houses, who make up the thousands of estates and villages in this country. We will only fulfil Jesus' command to go into all the world if we go into the world on our own doorstep.

Central to evangelism is church planting, which has been proven in different parts of the world as the most effective method of evangelizing. But it appears that thousands of churches remain unconvinced. Theology as the biblical basis for church planting has been explored in other books. This is a practical book giving details of the 'how'. I hope that many local churches who have never considered planting a church will find the seed thoughts here to begin the process. Although church planting is no longer a new idea, it stills feels out of reach to the majority of churches.

The challenge to evangelize through church planting has come from a number of sources, principally through the Holy Spirit who has stirred the Church to concentrate on this vital ministry. However, there are other factors. The vision of DAWN 2000, with its belief that the world can be reached by planting several million new churches, is one. DAWN stands for 'Discipling A Whole

Nation' and has been explained by Jim Montgomery in *Dawn 2000: 7 Million Churches to Go*.[1] It argues that denominations and local churches should set targets and then plant 'after their own kind'. This recognizes that each church has a distinctive contribution alongside others, each with a different ethos. It is committed to neighbourhood evangelism and believes that there should be a church for every 1,000 people. The new churches (previously known as house churches) have led the way over the last twenty years in church planting – notably, Ichthus (South-East London), Pioneer People (based in Surrey) and New Frontiers (Brighton).

More recently the ministry of Willow Creek Community Church in Chicago has come to the fore. Bill Hybels, Senior Pastor, began with three aims: firstly, to create a biblical community in which there would be transparent, loving relationships; secondly, a prime focus of reaching those who have no Christian commitment; and thirdly, unashamedly, inviting a high degree of commitment from those who follow Christ. The aim has been simplified: 'to turn irreligious people into fully devoted followers of Christ'. This concentration on the unchurched, especially with the decision to make Sunday a day for the unbeliever rather than the believer, has presented an incredible challenge to us.

In addition to this, Britain has become even more cosmopolitan in its make-up. The truth is that the Church is making virtually no impact on the ethnic minorities. Added to this we have large percentages of the population who feel culturally alienated from our churches for different reasons. Attempts have been made to counter this through adventurous churches like Kensington Temple, with its several ethnic satellite churches. And a number of new churches have been established in the country to reach a particular age group, especially young people, with a culturally relevant base. It is quite some time since Donald McGavran (church-growth specialist) presented us with the evidence that people were not always rejecting the Gospel, but the culture in which it was packaged. Hard thinking still needs to take place in this department if large sections of the population are to be reached.

Almost every denomination has decided that these last ten years of the millenium should be devoted to evangelism. Whereas we can so easily fall into the traditional response by planning local, regional or national missions, a far bigger strategy is required, with church planting as its prime aim. The nation needs evangelism of every type, but the bold and clear goal to reach every village, town and city by establishing culturally relevant and local congregations is fundamental.

THE VISION TO PLANT

HOW DOES IT COME ABOUT?

GO INTO ALL THE WORLD

A number of factors will cause a local church to think about planting, but the overriding reason must be evangelism. Jesus' command to 'Go into all the world and make disciples of all nations' remains central to ministry (Matthew 28:18-20). This commission is repeated in different ways in each of the gospels: 'Go into all the world and preach the good news to all creation' (Mark 16:15); 'Repentance and forgiveness of sins will be preached in His name to all nations' (Luke 24:47); 'As you have sent me into the world, I have sent them into the world . . . As the Father has sent me, I am sending you' (John 17:18 and 20:21).

Churches who are gripped by this incredible vision will be imaginative and effective in church planting. It's surprising how many of us can begin with the word 'go' and still base our outreach around the word 'come'. We are challenged by stirring sermons which clearly expound the imperative to go into all the world, and yet most of the events that are organized are centred on our church buildings. Clearly we are expecting people to come. Most of our church patterns advance the notion that we expect unbelievers to come and listen on our territory. Although 'go' is only a two-letter word it has tremendous power when relevantly obeyed. There is no short-circuiting of this fundamental responsibility.

OTHER FACTORS

Accepting that an evangelistic and 'going' mentality is primary, what are the indicators and questions that arise to trigger the initial thought of planting?

1 A FULL CHURCH

Church buildings vary in size and our vision can be limited to the number of seats. The church-growth people tell us that when the building is 80 per cent full it is time to plan changes. Some churches have been full, or nearly full, for months if not years. Action must take place. What are the choices?

- Begin a building programme to increase the seating capacity. As well as the high cost, as growth continues the same problem is to be faced at a later date.
- Hold a second morning service. This immediately doubles the number of people who can attend, but can have the disadvantage of drawing people away from their own communities to attend worship.
- Use the same building for very different congregations. St Thomas Crookes in Sheffield and the Elim, Kensington Temple in London are examples of this. This means that worshippers identify with a particular service, or an age group is targeted by providing a relevant programme.
- Plant a church elsewhere. This is the most adventurous and fruitful action to take, but requires more thought and planning to be effective.

A church may be full but not yet ready to plant. Creating the environment for a church planting ministry will take considerable time, and such churches want to grow in numbers in the meantime. In both churches where I have pastored we made the decision to develop two morning services before planting simply because the time was not right.

2 KNOWING THE STATISTICS

A town or city may have well-attended and lively churches. This may lift our spirits but blind us to some depressing statistics. The couple of thousand who regularly attend the churches are only about 10 per cent or less of the overall population. We have little reason to feel pleased with ourselves because, placed alongside the local population, we are barely scratching the surface. Statistical information is easily obtained from local libraries and the National Census. [1]

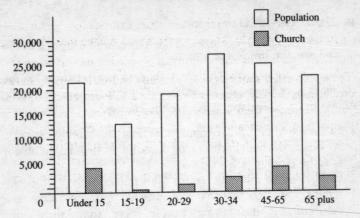

NB. Although a growing church in Guildford is reason to rejoice, it must be put into the context of 88 per cent of the population not attending church.

Fig. 1 *Guildford: age profile of church and population*[2]

Such information should stir the heart, enlarge the vision and inform the local church of the extent of the task. Coupled with this, accurate data concerning particular ages and social groupings is easily obtained and strategic targeting will result. For example, a youth survey in St Helens, *Youth – The Spoiling Harvest*[3], revealed disturbing facts from the Christian point of view. All attend a large comprehensive school.

- From eleven to thirteen years, 6-10 per cent of youth attend church once a week, but from fourteen years upwards, 0-1 per cent attended once a week.
- As teens get older a change occurred. The 'don't believe' population decreased, but the 'don't know' increased. The search has begun by the time they reach fifteen years old.
- 25 per cent indicated that friendships were the thing they liked most. Yet not one indicated that they were influenced about religion by their friends. There appears to be a great lack of positive peer pressure in regard to faith.
- Most of the lads were unwilling to associate themselves with any church. It damages their 'image' to identify with what they see as a group of 'olds'.

- There was no comprehension that 'church' has to do with people and lifestyle. Answers were always related to the building and not the life of the church.

These, and other statistics, led St Helens' church leadership to two conclusions. Firstly, there is a need for a relevant church life for youth. Secondly, there is a need for more workers to be thrust into the harvest. The idea of youth churches, or congregations within churches (services particularly relevant to young people), is being explored in a variety of places (The Gap in Swindon, The Brown Bear in London, The Joy Fellowship in Oxford, Interface – part of the Pioneer network, and The Warehouse in Guildford).

3 A NEW ESTATE

When the Church of England parish system was introduced, every person was considered because all the roads and farms were covered. Over the centuries thousands of new estates have been built which have simply increased numbers in each parish.

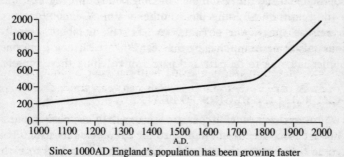

Since 1000AD England's population has been growing faster than the number of churches.

In the year 1000 there was one church for every 200 people.

In 1851 there was one church for every 500 people.

In 1989 there was one church for every 1,200 people.

Fig. 2   *England: population per church*[4]

Churches are often overlooked by the planners when a new estate is being built. The forward-looking church is challenged by the considerable increase in population on their doorstep. This may merely result in leafleting the new homes to introduce the churches or, alternatively, a more adventurous vision may emerge of a new church.

4 EVERYBODY'S DOING IT

We are all influenced through the experience of others. We hear the story of what the Baptists, URC or the Anglicans are doing in such and such a village, or on the new estate. There are now five church-planting churches in Guildford, whereas three years ago only the Guildford Community Church had taken the plunge. The body of Christ needs to be both encouraged and *challenged* by one another to take seriously what God is saying to us about these things.

The DAWN movement has greatly increased the awareness of denominations to the challenge of planting new churches. This has brought the matter onto all of our agendas, whether we like it or not. The Methodists agreed at their conference to plant a new church in every circuit (over 700). The Salvation Army have proposed 500 and the Assemblies of God 1,000 new congregations by the year 2000. Adding this to other mainline denominations, as well as the newer streams, we are talking about literally thousands of new churches by the year 2000. Learning from one another is going to be part and parcel of reaching these targets.

5 CHURCH LIFE BEGINS TO PLATEAU

It is proven that new churches grow faster than established ones. When a church has been established for a few years its structures become fixed rather than flexible. The ratio of members to each new convert is considerably higher in an established church than in a new one. One of the goals of West Bridgford Baptist Church in Nottingham, of which I was pastor, was forty converts during the year: twelve of these were to come from a church we had planted and twenty-eight from the main congregation. There were twenty three adults in the planted church and over 250 in the main church. At the end of the year we had recorded forty-two people who had made a commitment to Christ. The new church had reached their goal of twelve. There will always be exceptions to this rule depending on the leadership gifts and make-up of a particular church.

Finally, a church may begin to think about church planting through calling a new leader. He acts as a catalyst for vision and change.

IN WHAT SORT OF CHURCHES DOES IT OCCUR?

I have been describing what factors influence a church to *think* about planting, but what of those who believe God is leading them to move in this direction? The many different characteristics of church planting are covered in this book as a whole, but I wish to concentrate on two aspects in this section: the leadership group, and the development of vision and how the church members 'own' it.

1 WHAT SORT OF LEADERSHIP?

The effectiveness of any church is related to the quality of its leaders, even though some of us who occupy such positions would prefer it differently. What sort of leadership is characteristic in a planting church?

Sharing as a team

The 'one man band' leader will find it difficult to plant a church. By this I don't mean a church leader without other full-time members, but one who is not sharing the responsibility of ministry. If the leader has not learned to delegate his ministry to reliable people he will probably not be in favour of allowing a group from the church to plant elsewhere. It is in leadership teams that the broadest-based ministry is found, and together they lay the best foundation for extending outwards.

But what sort of team?

A good exercise is to analyse how your leadership group is gifted. Using Ephesians 4:11 as a base ask the question, 'Where does each leader's main contribution lie?' The gifts of Christ outlined in Ephesians are integral to a church planting ministry.

These ministries are gifts of Christ to build up and equip the Church, and to prepare God's people for Christian service.

Apostle: Literally meaning **one sent forth**. The desire to move outwards and onwards is integral to such a person. It also includes ministry across churches, foundation laying, and the exercise of governmental spiritual authority. (In the Church as a whole there is disagreement about the meaning of this gift.)

Prophet: Literally meaning **one who speaks forth a message from God**. This person is able to express the mind of God in order to guide, and sometimes warn. The message may come in a variety of ways: word, revelation, dream, vision, symbol.

Evangelist: Literally meaning **a messenger of good**. This is essentially good news about Jesus Christ and the Kingdom of God. They function within the church to encourage Christians outwards towards the world, and in society proclaiming Jesus as Lord leading to repentance and faith.

Pastor: Literally, **a shepherd**. All the functions of the shepherd with his sheep: tending, guarding, feeding, etc. Enabling the church to be a caring community, where love and truth are expressed.

Teacher: Literally, **one who instructs**. Able to expound and clarify the word of God in detail, in order to teach and train believers in the ways of God.

The early Church was founded on apostles and prophets, with Christ Jesus being the cornerstone (Ephesians 2:20). The prophets and teachers in Antioch were led by the Holy Spirit to send Paul and Barnabas to evangelize and plant churches (Acts 13:1-5). We read that 'Paul and Barnabas preached the good news and won large numbers of disciples. They returned to Lystra, Iconium and Antioch, strengthening the disciples and encouraging them to remain true to the faith . . . Paul and Barnabas appointed elders for them *in each church* and, with prayer and fasting, committed them to the Lord.' (Acts 14:21-23, my emphasis.) As we recover these ministries more progress will be made.

Often the main gift orientation is pastoral. Churches tend to elect the so-called 'safe' pastors and the 'helpful' teachers. The evangelist is left to serve at the edge of the church's life, the prophet considered a trouble-maker, and who are the apostles anyway? We have neglected church leadership that will move members outwards and give prophetic insight into God's heart for the community. It can be a frustrating place for an elder with evangelistic gifts, stirring the church to 'go', only to find the rest of the eldership undermining this thrust by giving a stronger emphasis to stay. The tension between building up members in their faith and expecting all to be evangelistic is a balance not easily achieved. The Church in this country has tended to emphasize the pastoral ministry and is only now coming to terms with its calling to mission.

If this outward and evangelistic policy is not at the heart of the leadership, the church will be unlikely to plant. It can lead to the more evangelistic within the membership deciding to act themselves, and this may lead to a church being planted due to a split. The leader of the team needs to know that the other members are at one with the aim of church planting, because pressures to deflect from the task will come both from within and outside the fellowship. There will always be those in churches who believe in evangelism in theory, but not in practice. And planting in another area involves the spiritual dimension of opposition from Satan. The powers of evil will try to weaken the leadership's resolve to plant, knowing it will affect the church as a whole.

Leaders with evangelistic hearts

The leaders of the Ichthus Christian Fellowship recognized at the founding of the church that each leader needed to have a high commitment to evangelism. Their long-term church planting programme in South-East London continues to thrive due to this common vision. But this is not the case in most of our churches. To fall into line with God's purpose of reaching this nation the following will help a leadership group:

- Ask God to increase your commitment to evangelism. Just as those of us who, being more evangelistically inclined, can ask for God's help to become more pastorally sensitive, I believe that it works in the opposite direction as well. God has given us His Holy Spirit (the Spirit of Jesus) and surely His plan is to make us like His Son. Jesus had the perfect blending of gifts and attitudes. I appreciate that not all have the same gift, but we can ask to be changed.

I suppose another way of expressing this is the challenge of a deepening relationship with God. This results in beginning to *feel* as well as *know* His love for the world. God has not stopped having strong compassion for the world that He created, and as we grow closer to Him, we will share His heart and longing for those who are not yet Christians.

- Make time to get alongside unbelievers or an evangelistic activity. The reality is that we are mixing with unbelievers all the time in different settings. The truth for many Christians is that the desire to share our faith is very low. Leaders need challenging to make time for, and increase their desire for witnessing. One of our elders decided to give Tuesday evenings over to football. He enjoys the game, but as well as physical exercise he has found a natural context to witness. For many in churches, becoming less committed to church activities and joining a secular evening club will pay dividends. You might say that this is obvious, but do you do it?

  I have done this through door-to-door visitation because I am interested in the people. There are legitimate reasons to visit: a local pastor/church leader wanting to introduce himself; a questionnaire – but only if you are truly wanting to know their thoughts; to inform about a series of special services; general visitation in preparation for a plant. Such visitation has produced a number of contacts and friends. Too many of us in the ministry spend almost all our time with Christians. Although there are obvious reasons for this, we also need the challenge and refreshment of non-churchy people.

- Look for the potential evangelistic leaders in the congregation. Who are the individuals who are fruitful in evangelism? Who are the people who bring friends to church and initiate evangelistic events? Who amongst these have leadership potential? Decide as a leadership to nurture and encourage them with a view to becoming part of the leadership team. An element of risk is being taken because they are not the safe pastoral types, but this is essential if the church is to share the same spirit.

● Receive input from another church. Local churches can be greatly helped, and changed, through the input of gifted leaders from another church. God intended us to be instructed through such wider church ministry (prophets, healers, teachers, apostles, evangelists, etc.). The new church streams, who have more whole-heartedly embraced these functions, have experience to impart to the mainline denominations.

Many new churches will only be planted by local churches being willing to be developed and envisioned by the apostolic and prophetic insights of leaders outside their fellowships. This implies that through trusting relationships we allow such leaders freedom to develop us. Due to our independence we often encourage folk from outside to 'come and bless us, but not to build amongst us'. It is, therefore, advisable to form relationships with one or more such leaders so that their ministry can be received in an ongoing way, and the church as a whole learns to receive from them. This enables the local leadership to grow in vision and ability and rise to a bigger challenge.

2 DEVELOPING VISION

How does a church decide on its vision? Where does it come from? How do we involve all the members? How do we help reluctant and fearful church members? In Nottingham our vision became clearer when we asked the question, 'What are the aspects of church life that are most fruitful?' If a church is praying and asking God to lead them, it is likely that there are already visionary things taking place.

We agreed as leaders that the four aspects requiring greater attention were housegroups, developing gifts and ministries, unity, and evangelism and church planting. Also, four foundation blocks of worship, prayer, obedience and encouragement were highlighted. A member put these into a drawing which the West Bridgford Baptist Church still uses today. It can be seen that the direction of the church points towards church planting. This demonstrates that church energies were to further this end.

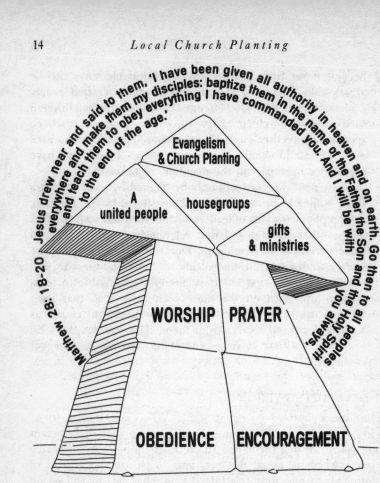

Jesus drew near and said to them, 'I have been given all authority in heaven and on earth. Go then to all peoples everywhere and make them my disciples: baptize them in the name of the Father the Son and the Holy Spirit and teach them to obey everything I have commanded you. And I will be with you always.' to the end of the age.'

Matthew 28: 18-20

Evangelism & Church Planting

A united people

housegroups

gifts & ministries

WORSHIP   PRAYER

OBEDIENCE   ENCOURAGEMENT

Fig. 3   Vision arrow

How did we know that these were the points to emphasize?

- We had grown in our number of housegroups and recognized the spiritual value of the small group. In a growing church the small unit is crucial.
- We knew that unity would be increasingly important as we took steps to move out from our central base.
- We were committed to every member serving appropriately and recognized the place of training and identifying people's gifts.
- We had begun working with a small group on the first plant and it was going well.

As a church identifies how to use its time it has the effect of sharpening up vision and each member sees more easily where they fit in. So how was this communicated to the membership, and how did they signify their agreement?

The church was divided into four sections in order to work with smaller groups. Individual members of each section were personally invited to attend on three successive Tuesday evenings, when the vision at the top of the arrow was explained. (The foundation blocks were taught during the Sunday morning teaching programme. Encouragement of one another was included because we had discovered its importance in our Christian service.) We explained in detail the different aspects of the vision and opportunity was given on each occasion to ask the hard questions. We wanted members to be both clear about and in agreement with what was planned. During the final session we assessed whether they were ready to commit themselves.

A church membership must own the way forward for themselves. This is unlikely to be unanimous because some will require a longer period of time to be convinced. However, the larger body of the membership should be giving both their agreement and support otherwise it will flounder.

At those initial meetings a few places were mentioned as possible plants. Almost all of them now have a congregation serving these areas. To give the membership plenty of time to get used to the thought of a plant in a particular area sows the seed and roots the idea. This usually results in quicker acceptance when firmer plans are being made.

QUESTIONS TO FACE

When the vision of planting becomes more than just a good idea, members need reassurance concerning a number of different matters. The vision won't take root in the church until members believe they have been adequately informed and their hesitations dealt with. What are the likely objections and how do we overcome them?

In the 1980s the question was raised, 'Should we plant out or become a larger central church?' The church was devolved into areas but all the work still based at the centre.

1990 In the calling of a new pastor, experience of church planting was considered to be a significant factor.

1991 (March) Agreement by elders that church planting was the right course.

(April/May) Shared with wider leadership group to answer questions and sharpen the vision.

(June) Presentation of the vision to the wider membership including:

- Biblical basis
- Types of church planting
- What is the method for Millmead?
- How are we to do it?

This was recorded on video and several copies made. Over the next few months they were used either personally or within housegroups. This meant that members could have adequate time to understand and to share with one another.

(November) The church business meeting was devoted almost entirely to talking through implications of planting. The general consensus was to adopt church planting as the next stage for Millmead.

1 'LET US FILL OUR EXISTING BUILDING FIRST'

Hundreds of churches are far from full and thoughts of church planting seem not only remote but impossible. This usually ends the argument for many church members. We are too dominated by the buildings that we call church. Biblically speaking, churches are made up of individuals who have repented and believe in Jesus Christ as Lord. It might be that our building was built to hold 500, and the 200 who attend look small in comparison. Finding a more acceptable room in which to worship is both more practical and psychologically more helpful. A section of the 200 may travel several miles from another village or town and can be encouraged to explore possibilities there.

The church building in Nottingham held about 400 and after

several congregations had been sent out, it felt too large for those who remained. For six months we agreed to worship in the church hall. This resulted in deeper fellowship and new growth. When the hall was outgrown we returned to the church, but did so with a completely different attitude.

We have to recover the New Testament truth that church is about people. We can express our worship and witness anywhere. The truth is that for the first 200 years of the Church there were no church buildings.

2 'IT WILL SPOIL RELATIONSHIPS WITH OTHER CHURCHES'

Some members, anxious to maintain good relationships with other local churches, will be slower to embrace church planting. In ecumenical days this is an important consideration. Actually, in reality, it can hold up a church planting strategy a very long time.

A strength of DAWN 2000 is the principle of 'planting after your own kind'. For too long we have struggled to find organic unity, and generally failed. If we maintain good attitudes and a spirit of encouragement towards other local churches, rather than competition, there is room for several different churches in a given area. Before a plant begins on a Sunday, and preferably before a final decision is made about where the plant is to be, local churches should be consulted. My experience is that there are few difficulties when this procedure is followed. What is more interesting is that the other local churches often raise their mission profile as a result of the new church.

Arrange to meet with the local clergy or at least talk on the telephone. In a relaxed setting questions are answered and often misconceptions are removed. So many barriers and misunderstandings are overcome through this approach. What is not negotiable is the commitment to plant and evangelize. However it may be that, through this process, timing or other aspects will alter. Or it may be discovered that another church is also thinking about a plant in that area and efforts may be fruitfully combined. My desire is that the unbelievers are reached – I am not too bothered who reaches them. There is enough work for all of us

Check List

Most barriers will be overcome if you:

1 Telephone or send a letter to make initial contact.

2 Attend a local fraternal of clergy, if there is one.

3 Explain reasons for wanting to church plant:

a) Evangelism not sheep-stealing. Try to centre the discussion around mission.

b) Concentration on a particular neighbourhood, probably where there is no church presence.

c) Another expression of the Body of Christ in the locality, not a take-over bid.

d) Tackle the delicate issue of some Christians who wish to be involved in this sort of evangelism transferring churches. If this happens, suggest how it will be handled most helpfully.

e) The community will understand the planting of a new church if we support one another's churches.

f) Encourage honest sharing.

4 Keep the other churches informed about progress.

5 Provide them with any literature that will be delivered, prior to delivery.

and we need not duplicate. If members know that this dialogue is taking place they are reassured.

3 'IS THIS THE LATEST CRAZE?'

Like the Athenians (Acts 17), we are always wanting something new. The latest church programme will be the panacea for all our ills. Some will want to know if this is simply the latest new idea. I do not believe so.

Church planting is thoroughly biblical. I don't intend to present a great deal of theological material on this point, because it has been given in great depth in other books (e.g. *Planting Tomorrow's Churches Today* by Robinson and Christine[5]; *Radical Church Planting* by Ellis and Mitchell[6]). Jesus had little to say about planting churches. He certainly referred to the existence of the Church in Matthew's gospel (Matthew 16:18; 18:17), but gave no clear strategy. However, He did command the disciples to take up the great commission as we have seen, which would inevitably lead to the establishing of churches.

The book of Acts records the history and development of church planting. Jesus said, 'You shall receive power when the Holy Spirit shall come upon you; *and you will be my witnesses in Jerusalem, Judea, Samaria, and to the ends of the earth.*' (Acts 1:8) But the apostles were reliant on the leading of the Spirit as to how this would be fulfilled. The message was taken from Jerusalem, through Samaria, to the centre of large populations: Antioch, Ephesus, Athens, Corinth and Rome. It was from these bases that the surrounding regions were reached. There must have been many different congregations in these large cities.

For the early Church, like ourselves, it was the command to evangelize that was the springboard, which inevitably led to the formation of the communities of believers. Similarly today, as we face up to the fact of 40 million unchurched people in the British Isles, the Gospel will create churches where it is proclaimed. History informs us of the church planting that follows in the wake of revivals. I was a Methodist for twenty-six years and often reflect on the success of the denomination in being able to plant and build in so many villages and towns.

4 'ONE CHURCH IS EASIER TO RESOURCE AND MAINTAIN'

A local church that is running well brings its own satisfaction. Churches need good organization: leaders in place, members knowing what their roles are, the youth and children's ministry well-catered for, an exciting programme, etc., etc. Why rock the boat by suggesting starting *another* church? It will involve more finance – hire of buildings and possibly employment of a new staff member. It will mean facing questions of who is to go and who is to stay, and who is going to do all the jobs.

Planting another church will cause a certain amount of upheaval but raises a whole host of good questions as well. What is the church here for? Have we been spending too much time on teaching and fellowship? Who are the members who are longing to be used but have little opportunity to do so? Where should the pastor/priest/minister be spending his time — at home or away? What is the level of faith in what God can do?

This is why we require an evangelistic vision at the church's heart. The Christian ministry requires us to have big plans for those who are not yet Christians. Our churches were never intended to become comfortable places catering for just our needs. Of course we will need to adequately feed the sheep and build up the faith, but always remember Archbishop Temple's words about 'the church existing for those who don't yet belong to it'.

5 'WHAT HAPPENS IF IT FAILS?'

Some church plants have not been successful. The fear of failure is very powerful and has caused many a church leadership to hold back. I am so glad that there has been a spirit of adventure in the two churches to which I have belonged. It is because we have tried and sometimes failed that there is now greater confidence to do it right.

The reluctance to tackle new territory goes back as far as the Israelites in the Wilderness. Numbers 13 and 14 speak clearly to today's situation. Which of the twelve spies are we like? After they returned from exploring Canaan the report went as follows:

We went into the land to which you sent us, and it does flow with milk and honey! Here is its fruit. But the people who live there are powerful, and the cities are fortified and very large. We even saw descendants of Anak there. The Amalekites live in the Negev; the Hittites, Jebusites and Amorites live in the hill country; and the Canaanites live near the sea and along the Jordan. (Numbers 13:27–29)

Certainly it is difficult territory for us — spiritual forces opposing us, apathy and probably rejection from a percentage of the people, and hard work for the planting group. But the Israelites were wrong and they missed the opportunity. Fear always has more to say than faith. Notice Caleb's words: 'We should go and take possession of the land because we can certainly do it.' (Numbers 13:30)

We need to unmask this issue for what it is. We are called to faith, and to believe that with God's help we can do it. Of course, good preparation is essential and we should be aware of what can go wrong if there are no solid foundations.

WHAT MAKES A GOOD PLANTER?

Before we discuss the qualifications of leaders, a brief survey of some Old and New Testament characters and their qualities will provide a biblical framework. Leaders of new churches would do well to emulate the 'spirit' that characterized them.

PIONEER: ABRAHAM

'The Lord had said to Abraham, "LEAVE your country, your people, and your father's household and go to the country I WILL SHOW YOU".' (Genesis 12:1) Abraham was a man on the move but unsure of where he was going. He was the man of faith, ready and willing to pioneer new territory (Hebrews 11:8). He would be blessed and bring blessing to those who encountered him (Genesis 12:2–3).

It is the pioneering spirit, with strong faith, which desires to bless the world as well as the church. The pioneering leader will motivate people to leave the mother church and move into a plant.

BOLDNESS: JOSHUA

'I will give you EVERY PLACE WHERE YOU SET YOUR FOOT, as I promised Moses. Be STRONG and COURAGEOUS, because you will lead these people to inherit the land.' (Joshua 1:3, 6) Joshua had been well prepared by Moses during the long trials of the Wilderness. He had, with Caleb, agreed that the land was possible to take. He had received the Holy Spirit through the laying on of Moses' hands (Deuteronomy 34:9). He was now hearing God's voice that it was time to act with boldness.

This was not boldness based on human power or experience. 'Strong' means to lay hold of God's strength, and 'courageous' means to hold on firmly once you have started.

BUILDER: NEHEMIAH

'Then Nehemiah said to them, "You see the trouble we are in: Jerusalem lies in ruins, and its gates have been burned with fire. LET US REBUILD THE WALL." They replied, "LET US START REBUILDING." So they began this good work.' (Nehemiah 2:17–18) Nehemiah had been burdened by the news of Jerusalem. He freed himself to get to his beloved city, spied out the land and then exercised his gift of building. We recognize that behind his obvious gifts of inspiration and working with people he had a passion for God's name to be honoured.

It begins with Nehemiah, but soon the people will be giving their verbal commitment and time to building the wall. Chapter 3 inspires us with the picture of each one playing their part.

IDENTIFICATION: ISAIAH

'"Woe to me!" Isaiah cried. "I am ruined! For I AM A MAN OF UNCLEAN LIPS, AND I LIVE AMONG A PEOPLE OF UNCLEAN LIPS, and my eyes have seen the King, the Lord Almighty." The Lord said, "Go and tell this people." ' (Isaiah 6:5, 9) Isaiah received God's forgiveness which he would proclaim to his fellow sinful nation. He went as a messenger, aware of the holiness and requirements of God, but also inviting his hearers to 'turn to the Lord, because He will have mercy, and to God, for He will freely pardon' (Isaiah 55:7).

The ability to identify with the community with whom we are sharing is a mark of God's grace and follows Jesus' example in His incarnation.

PROPHECY: HAGGAI

'The WORD OF THE LORD CAME THROUGH HAGGAI to Zerubbabel, governor of Judah, and to Joshua, the high priest.' (Haggai 1:1) Haggai brought God's word about priorities. This meant working on the temple and not on their own homes (1:2–11). In one of the shortest biblical prophecies he assured them that God was with them (1:13). And he exhorted them to be strong and work because the future glory was going to be much better than the past (2:1–9).

Listening to God's voice is an indispensable ingredient in the establishing of new churches.

MISSION: JESUS

'Jesus said, "Let us go somewhere else — to the nearby villages — so that I can preach there also. That is why I have come." So He travelled through Galilee, preaching in their synagogues and driving out demons.' (Mark 1:38–39) Many different qualities could be applied to the Lord Jesus, but it was His sense of mission that dominated His life. He knew why He had been sent, and He wanted to finish the work that the Father had given Him (John 4:34). He resisted the temptation to remain at Capernaum, where His ministry was proving so successful. The disciples told Him, 'Everyone is looking for you!' (Mark 1:37), but it was time to move on. He had heard the new instructions very early that morning (Mark 1:35).

STRATEGY: PAUL

Paul wrote, 'It has always been my ambition to preach the Gospel where Christ was not known, so that I would not be building on someone else's foundation.' (Romans 15:20) As we follow Paul through the Acts of the Apostles we see his strategy of wanting to bring Christianity to the main centres of population on his way to Rome.

It would appear that to be a strategist is a God-given ability. Compared with what Paul and the early apostles achieved in the first thirty years, what has followed in the last 1,900 leaves much to be desired.

THE LEADER IS THE KEY

There is world-wide agreement that the leader is the key to the success of a new church. To make the wrong choice means that the church will either fold up or lose its sense of outreach. To state it crudely, there are some who can make it happen and some who can't. In this I am not speaking of human charisma, but those appropriately gifted by God. I believe that it is possible to develop the right qualities in a potential leader, so don't set aside a person too quickly.

A number of leaders who desire to plant are too pastoral in their gifting. This often results in a caring family church, which has little motivation to introduce new people. Jesus said, 'They will know you are Christians by the way you love one another.' (John 13:34–35) Therefore, we need to have unbelievers among us for them to notice.

I remember talking to a man, in the early stages of one plant, who clearly thought of himself as the natural choice to lead. It was important for me to make it clear at that stage that I did not see the qualities in him to lead the work. I believed his leadership gifts to be more pastoral than evangelistic. However, I also said that I would try to develop him. It has been a joy to recognize a growing commitment in his life to the community, and leadership that inspires the members to go out.

HOW DO YOU DEVELOP POTENTIAL LEADERS?

- The experienced planter should share himself. He should make clear what is important to him and why. Potential leaders learn a great deal from the example of others; it is caught as well as taught. They will begin to understand how the planter thinks, and why God has led them to hold certain convictions.
- The ability to think and act evangelistically has to be cultivated. Suggest practical ways of doing this by getting involved with people and events which will test and stretch their faith.
- When the trainee has a good idea or a sense of direction, allow him to present it to the congregation and experience what is required in bringing good ideas into reality.
- Time needs to be given to the trainee on a one-to-one basis in prayer, discipling and encouragement.
- Gently point out areas of weakness and encourage personal growth.

It will become clear whether or not the person has the ability to be the leader on his own.

A church needs to wait until the right leader is available before they embark, even though there will be strong pressures from members to begin. The average church member tends to believe that the work is going to be successful 'once something starts in their locality'. This sort of simplistic thinking must be corrected (see Chapter 3).

QUALIFICATIONS FOR THE LEADER

On one occasion I attended a workshop on the subject of 'What makes a good planter?' We were asked to give a list of characteristics and qualities needed in the right man or woman. Well over twenty were listed and at that point I decided we were looking for Superman. In some textbooks an equally formidable list appears, but I believe there are five aspects that the aspiring church planter requires. I will use the pronoun 'he', but this ministry is also for women.

1 PASTOR—EVANGELIST

The planter is leading a group of Christians and his purpose is to expand the church by conversion growth. If the person is too strongly evangelistic, the shaping and nurturing of the new church will fall short and necessary aspects of a wholesome church life will, therefore, be missing. If, as has been implied earlier, the pastoral predominates, the cutting edge into the community goes by the board.

Such folk must be identified within our churches and trained accordingly, but there are also many pastors fulfilling the traditional role who have the ability to plant churches. They may have experienced a certain amount of frustration, in that they feel saddled with too much in-church ministry and long to be free to make more strategic advances into their communities. It is not easy to resolve this dilemma, but I believe many more of us will have to grapple with this tension so that more new churches can be established.

The planter needs to be willing to take responsibility for the church to grow and not think this is the job for someone else. He thinks, dreams and prays for growth, and has a heightened desire to want people to become part of the church family. In some circles this individual is known as a 'break-through' person. As the name

Gedling Baptist Church was launched at the Grey Goose Public House by the Westdale Lane Baptist Church, Nottingham. It was agreed by the church that Graham Coventry, Senior Pastor, should lead this new work.

Graham chose to spearhead the pioneer work himself for a number of reasons. He had the personal call from God for this particular task and also the vision of where to plant. In addition, the congregation experienced and recognized their pastor's gifts as evangelistic and apostolic.

When the congregation together faced the problem of overcrowding some six years previously the issue of church planting had been a very real option. However, they received a clear word from the Lord, 'Do not plant yet'. Instead, they extended their building and strengthened the leadership by calling elders and a second pastor. During this time of taking practical steps they did not lose sight of the vision of church planting and were ready to embark upon such a project when the time was right.

The spiritual responsibility for being 'team leader' for the two fellowships, but remaining one church, still lies with Graham. However, John Davies and the elders have taken on the day-to-day running of the mother church and its pastoral care. Graham supervises the new church in Gedling, working alongside his growing congregation. The initial core group was fifteen. But the leadership team intend to strengthen the eldership still further

implies, it is someone who has the spiritual ability to break through into a community with a sense of Christ. The prospect of establishing a new church is remote and quite out of the reach of most Christians. The planter sees the potential for reaching a community because of the way that he has been equipped by the Lord. The planter is certainly not content that the church should grow by transfers of Christians from other churches. He wants a church where the non-Christian can sense the relevance of Christ.

2 ENABLER

The desire to enable individual Christians to serve the Lord is a high priority. This is the only way that any lasting impact will be made on the community. It was never intended that we have a few with the inclusion of another elder, and in faith are looking towards appointing a youth pastor for the mother church. At present they are in the process of equipping and appointing a lay pastor for the church plant to work alongside Graham and the other leaders. Depending on how things develop, a full-time pastor for Gedling could be an addition to the team at some future date.

Pioneer work has not been without personal difficulties. Although the church has been supportive of him, Graham has had to face what he describes as a time of bereavement, as he relinquished many of his roles to John. The Lord has challenged him on where his security lies — in his position or in the Lord Himself. His intention is to bring the new church to a state of self-sufficiency so that he can take another group and start somewhere else.

The church recognizes the advantages of a pastor acting as planter. It gives the project authenticity rather than being thought of as a group of radicals doing their own thing. Pastors have a wide experience of church life to draw from and they are available to work full-time. In general, ministers from other churches respond more favourably to an ordained minister. But perhaps most important to Graham is the fact that a church planting ministry releases those in the church with evangelistic gifts, who find themselves in pastoral ministry with little opportunity to use this specific ability.

above-average Christians, but that all of us should come to maturity in our service for the Lord. But what sort of enabling? To equip the Body of Christ is the responsibility of all leaders, but there are four aspects to consider in the church planter context.

- To value other people's ministry as much as, or more than, his own: the only way that the work will be accomplished is by every member playing their part. The planter is not on an ego trip, concerned that others should admire his abilities. He is aware that, although this leads to personal appreciation for all that he does, it is missing the mark. He is most encouraged when others begin to serve the Lord effectively. This will mean that he is on the look-out for how the different gifts can be used.
- To model how to do different aspects of the work: The

members of the congregation will grow in confidence as they are shown how to serve. Door-to-door visiting may not recruit many volunteers initially, but when this is explained and time spent with folk on the doorsteps, the fear is taken out of the exercise.

Leading a service in a way that is free from Christian jargon and enabling the congregation to be at ease can also be modelled. A readiness to develop relationships with non-Christians, sharing the reasons and ways of doing this, gives the work a sense of reality. Also to lead in practical ways, like putting out the chairs and clearing away afterwards, helps to create the atmosphere of all of us being servants.

- To take risks with people and encourage them to have a go: After our most recent plant began a Bible study was organized for a group made up of mainly non-Christians. I led it with another member and after the first couple of meetings had other calls on my time, which meant I could not be present on every occasion. It meant that the helper was thrown in at the deep end. She did very well, not least because she had the love and respect of the people whom she had come to know over a period of a few months. The ability to give Christians a sense of confidence to do evangelistic-type ministry is an important quality in the planter.

- To have an eye for the person to lead after him: The planter will want to do himself out of a job in due course. He will be looking for his successor, who can lead the work in his absence. He will give this person opportunity to grow under his supervision, and he will spend time in one-to-one relationship to encourage.

If there is conviction that the trainee will be able to take responsibility for the work, the planter will raise that person's profile in the congregation and tell them that he is grooming him to take over when he eventually leaves, or as he becomes less involved. The trainee isn't being imposed, because it will be clear through consultation that the man is beginning to be recognized as a leader and has the respect of the group. There are obvious disadvantages of simply imposing a person from outside without consultation.

A group of churches in Reading have been running an evangelism training course under the name Ditchdiggers. The name is taken from 2 Kings 3:16, when God told the people through Elisha to dig ditches in preparation for the water He would send. Ditchdiggers came out of God's revealed strategy for the area. At its centre was a co-ordinated programme of church planting right across the region, planting congregations of live worshipping, believing Christians in every community. The programme continues to be directed and run by leaders of all participating churches who meet together regularly in this capacity.

Over the years Ditchdiggers has expanded in numbers and vision. Perhaps its unique aspect is that many of its participants are members of local Reading churches and it exists primarily to evangelize that one town and surrounding district. Currently the leaders represent nine churches, which together have twenty-two congregations and are still growing.

The one-year course takes in a full Bible survey and practical subjects, with students being assigned to different teams according to their gifting. One such would be a church planting team located in any one of the Ditchdigger network of churches or a street evangelism team. A third team specializes in schools presentations. The students also spend ten days of the year abroad on mission. Each person has to raise money to cover their own support throughout the year.

If we are going to meet the needs of an extensive church planting programme in this country a great deal of the training of our leaders will have to take place in a local setting rather than on a lengthy college course. There are, however, shorter courses available which are more accessible for busy people. (See Appendix A for details of appropriate training courses available.)

3 VISIONARY AND STRATEGIST

As with all leaders, a sense of vision for God's possibilities is essential in order to survive. However, alongside this vision of wanting to fulfil the great commission comes a strategy of how it is to be achieved.

The planter is a strategist. He does not just have a vague idea of what to do, stepping out in faith and hoping for the best. He is able to articulate the plan of the campaign, in the short-, medium- and long-term. He communicates to the group what is expected of them and some of the ways it is to be achieved. I say some of the ways, because he knows that the Holy Spirit will want to lead people individually and will be complementing the existing plan in effective ways. Therefore, setting clear goals and the ability to give direction are crucial to the congregation maintaining a sense of momentum and receiving encouragement from what is being achieved.

4 COMMITTED TO MOTHER–CHURCH LEADERSHIP

The planter is in good relationship with the sending church. If he has an independent spirit the work will quickly take on its own identity, and probably be built around the new leader. In some churches this has happened, although the original idea of the planting church was for an ongoing closer relationship. (This is covered in more detail in Chapter 7).

The planter is working on behalf of the sending church and values highly his fellow leaders. He wishes to maintain the unity of the Spirit and, because of a good relationship, opens the door to both encouragement and resources from the planting church. So qualities of loyalty and respect, humility and submissiveness, are the virtues that serve the overall work and provide the best atmosphere for decisions to be made.

5 PERSEVERANCE

The new plant will not succeed unless its leader has decided to see the task through. The Christian life generally is full of potential discouragements and hardships that make us want to give up. The planter will have many more personal and congregational obstacles to overcome. They fall into the following categories:

- Maintaining a motivation towards the world when it is far easier to concentrate on Christian fellowship and family.
- Recognizing that they are a main target of demonic attack, because to discourage the leader issues a severe blow to the whole work.

- Remaining God-centred when others in the group are discouraged or are not as committed as they initially indicated. Many times there is temptation to be discouraged and it is the inner strengthening of a relationship with God that will sustain him.
- When a congregational member brings pressure to alter the vision or the nature of the new church, to concentrate on teaching or fellowship, the planter will need to lovingly stand firm. Teaching is crucial, but the outward-looking aspect of the work needs to remain central.

To cope with these pressures the leader needs to learn to spiritually 'strengthen himself in God'. This is what is recorded of King David in 1 Samuel 30:6. He had been deserted by his men and now could rely on the Lord alone. It is the ability to look to God that will sustain personal motivation. I am not suggesting that there is no human support, but describing what is necessary when life is spiritually tough.

IS IT A FULL-TIME JOB?
Should it be a full-time position? Here are some of the responses from people who are presently planting churches.

1 *Do you think the position is your full-time work?*
'Not at present, the plant is not yet large enough to warrant full-time staff. However, I do give it a minimum of two days each week.'

'Not at present, although it has the potential to grow more quickly and then it should take a major part of my time.'

'Yes.'

Conclusion: It is clear that some planters believe that as the work grows they will need to give more of their time to it. I am sure this has been the case where lay leaders have become full-time pastors. But I wonder if more time is needed in the early stages of a plant, especially if we are training and delegating aspects of the work.

2 *What jobs do you oversee in your capacity as leader?*

'Leadership team, administration, Sunday and mid-week meetings, prayer, finance, children's work, pastoral care.'

'Overall leadership of the plant, worship team, care group leaders, Sunday services and weekly prayer meeting.'

'Visiting, services, children's work and administration.'

'Administration, overall leadership, pastoral care, monthly core group mid-week meeting, strategy group meetings, all other areas are delegated.'

Conclusion: The day-to-day running of activities seem to take much of the plant leader's time initially. This may ease if delegation to other members of the plant is effected.

3 *What aspects would you cover if you had more time?*

'Personal discipling and releasing ministry in others, more involvement in the community.'

'Outreach programme, helpline, pastoral.'
'More emphasis on visiting, small groups for evangelism.'

'Visitation of good contacts, more time in community, time to train and encourage those exercising key leadership.'

Conclusion: Leaders expressed a desire to spend more time in people-reaching and people-training areas. This emphasizes again that leaders should have the time to raise their profile in the community and not to be tied down by jobs that could be carried out by others.

4 *What resources from the sending church are available to you?*

'Offices, finance, personal support.'

'Finance, prayer support, administration, preachers.'

'Preachers, people for the congregation, children's workers, musicians, worship leaders, prayer support, keyboard, lecterns, hymn books.'

'Finance, administration, PA and OHP, prayer support.'

Conclusion: Mostly the resources were financial (including equipment) and spiritual (prayer and moral support), but in some cases there were quite large people resources involved, particularly initially. It is interesting to note that when asked how important these resources were, the basic answer was 'Vital!' with a stress on the importance of the moral and prayer support.

WOMEN IN LEADERSHIP

Two of the leaders planting churches in Guildford are women. I was interested to find out how they perceived their role and whether it was affected by their gender. The insights from Pauline Boland, leader of Park Barn Community Church, were particularly helpful:

1 *What tensions have you experienced leading the plant (i.e. because you're a woman)?*

'There have been many tensions over the few years since leading the church, some of which would have been common to both men and women, but these I think are particular to being a woman:

- 'Assurance of God's call to begin with. Surely God isn't asking me to do this, women don't do these things — these were my objections to start with!

- 'Self-confidence. Many women struggle with a sense of inferiority and in a situation which is traditionally male dominated this is more acute. Apart from the emotional difficulty, this area is a vulnerable one which our spiritual enemies attack and undermine.

- 'I (and I think most women) find serving and taking a supportive role natural. I've struggled within myself to maintain the overall leadership responsibility. I could easily defer to men and abdicate the responsibility which comes with the call.

- 'I think that at the beginning it was harder for us to feel we were a valid church. I expect most church plants have some sort of process to go through to find their identity, but to have all that plus being led by a woman makes it harder. Even though most of the church have no difficulty with the principle it can feel strange to begin with, added to which acceptance by other churches is important in knowing who we are and fully operating as part of the Body of Christ.

- 'In a similar way to the point made above, other churches found it hard to view us as a church rather than an extended housegroup or evangelism group. There were no other models of church planting in the town at the time, so two important principles were highlighted simultaneously. This type of thing all adds to the personal stresses and the need to keep focused on God.

- 'How to inspire men in the church? They need role models too. I had to come to realize that all men aren't natural leaders. Their role models don't have to be in a leadership position. The mature people, both men and women, in the church play an important part in helping others to grow in their relationship with God.

  'I see my role as encouraging men to develop the individual qualities God has given them, including leadership if that's there, but with no particular expectation that they will take the lead. I hope this is releasing to them. This tension has been felt by me and some of the men in the church, and by commitment to one another this is being worked out. Having said this, most of the men aren't aware enough of the difficulty to have faced it head on, it's more obvious in retrospect.

- 'Women have sometimes found it hard to have a woman leading. Some have felt threatened because they can't hide in traditional female roles (if it's OK for me then it's OK for them). Fears and insecurities have sometimes caused reactions.

- 'At home my husband has never shown any sign of finding my leading the church difficult, except when he once had a position of responsibility in the core group. It was hard for me to treat him the same as all the others in terms of what I expected of him. It was hard for him not to expect special treatment (reminders, prior warning, etc.). In trying not to show favouritism, I think I was very hard on him.

  'This was a difficult patch but has been a very beneficial experience both for us and our two children (a boy and a girl). We've learned the importance of being ourselves rather than stereotypes. The children have unusual role models and are open to possibilities for themselves, which may have seemed odd otherwise. Interestingly, my husband is still seen as the head of our family even though practically he does a lot of chores and I'm out a great deal doing other things.'

2 *What do you think are the advantages/disadvantages?*
'The advantages:

- 'People skills. A concern for and understanding of what makes people tick.
- 'Ability to think about several things at once.
- 'Approachable.' (Note: the comment from another female church planter on this point was that in door-to-door visitation, a woman is perceived as far less threatening than a man.)
- 'Available (more women are available to do the work involved in church planting).
- 'Servant hearts.
- 'Endurance.
- 'People rather than project-orientated.
- 'Listening skills. Applies to hearing God as well as people. I don't mean men can't hear God – I think women listen more readily.

'The disadvantages:

- 'History – expectations to overcome in self and others.
- 'No automatic respect of ability.
- 'The need to prove ourselves.
- 'Spiritual opposition peculiar to women:
  a) area of reproduction (physical and emotional);
  b) a particular enmity between Satan and women (Genesis 3:15);
  c) the need in men to rule women – a spiritual element as well as other reasons.
- 'Physical weaknesses:
  a) being seen in a crowd;
  b) projecting the voice;
  c) church planting can be physically demanding – moving

equipment, etc. 'We are dependent on men for some of this. (This is more a limitation than a disadvantage – we need to be interdependent.)

• 'Role models are few for women in leadership and we can easily begin to do things the way a man would and to value the traditionally male qualities rather than bring our own female qualities in.'

3 *Any other pearls of wisdom?*

'I actually feel that the differences are very few between men and women and that we should expect much more from both sexes. Concentration on the differences has, I feel, been limiting for us all.

'Our understanding of each other and our expectations need to be based on what God is saying rather than our fears or preconceptions. Let's all break out of whatever limits are not imposed on us by God. No one else has the right to do it and our spiritual enemies have a vested interest in limiting what God can do through us all, both men and women.'

THE LEADER AND THE TEAM

Although I have emphasized the necessity of the leader, he will be most effective in the context of a team. If he is wise he will recognize his need of those with gifts which complement his own. The direction of evangelism must not be compromised, but other significant gifts also require prominence. In his team, some of the following would be helpful:

• Teacher: The person to take responsibility for both Sunday teaching and the teaching needs of nurturing new Christians in any mid-week activity.

• Pastor–Evangelist (in embryo): Such a person should have strong leadership gifts and may well be the one to continue after the initial planter has moved on. Some visionary leaders tire if they are not presented with a new challenge regularly. Stickability is obviously an important virtue to cultivate, but it would appear that some members of the body are called to pioneer new work regularly.

- Worship Leader: The person to oversee the music group and plan appropriate worship.
- Administrator: The person to oversee the necessary administration and communication, and also to guide in practical ways the decisions being made.

It is advisable that this group should meet reasonably frequently in order to plan.

THE MIX OF GIFTS OVERALL

The people resources of each church or network of churches will vary greatly, as will also the emphases and type of churches we are wishing to create. There is not going to be a perfect set of individuals at the outset. Charlie Cleverly in *Church Planting – Our Future Hope* [1] sums up the Pioneer's Network Church Planting programme in this way. He has described it as their recipe:

1 Take one key leader, a 'break-through person'
2 Target an area in prayer and reasearch.
3 Take fifteen to twenty-five Christians of different gifts and abilities, especially including evangelists and healers.
4 Move to the area in question.
5 Evangelize by friendship and by high-profile healing meetings.
6 Add a small full-time, short-term training team.
7 Retain close ties with home base, keep in contact.
8 Stir in prayer.
9 Wait expectantly for explosion in the oven.

WHAT SORT OF PEOPLE DON'T YOU WANT?

In an article by Mike Hearn, 'Planting People, the Human Factor', [2] the following are listed:

1 Those who are malcontents, who have fallen out with other churches over secondary personality issues, rather than Gospel or theological issues.
2 Those whose personal or spiritual lives are a shambles.
3 Those with no time or energy to give to the church.

4 Those whose personal, social or emotional problems are such that the church is going to be sucked dry before it can get off the ground.

5 Those who are prejudiced and judgemental.

6 Those with very fixed ideas about everything.

He continues, 'Obviously it is impossible to make blanket rules about who should or shouldn't be involved. Every situation is different. But these are the areas I believe require careful attention.'

Bearing in mind all that has been said about leaders and the team, the following sort of people need to be identified:

- Are there a sufficient number of the more evangelistic Christians? If there is a local church planting school, these may be supplemented by students in training (e.g. Ditchdiggers in Reading).
- Are there those who will be able to oversee the children's ministry?
- Is there a musician or musicians who will accompany the worship adequately?
- Are there folk representing each age group? In one of our congregations we were short on older people and so two ladies were specifically asked to be members of the group for the first few months. A number of elderly people soon joined, but having their age group represented was initially very helpful.
- In contrast to the ones that are not suitable, such folk need to be characterized by their faith, enthusiasm, perseverance, reliability, a sense of humour and learning the centrality of God's love.

three

LAYING FOUNDATIONS

This chapter addresses two main points. Firstly, what follows when a decision has been made to plant, but before the planting team has been selected? And secondly, how to prepare the group who will form the core congregation, before starting regularly on a Sunday.

CHECK LIST: WHAT HAS HAPPENED SO FAR?

1 The leader(s) has a vision for church planting.
2 The idea of church planting is explained to the church.
3 The idea has become more of a reality and has begun to be owned by church members. Even though local church government varies (i.e. decisions made by elders, church council or congregation as a whole), it is important to bring as many members as possible on board so that they own it.
4 Research to discover where the plant is to take place. This includes spiritual direction through prayer as well as practical fact-finding (see Chapter 5).
5 Conviction from the Holy Spirit to plant in a particular locality.

Note: This process can take anything from two to five years, so don't become despondent.

WHO IS GOING TO JOIN THE TEAM?

At this stage it may not be absolutely clear that a particular locality is to have a new church. Often part of the guidance is to consult with those who will be involved. The location in question will have been in the mind of the church for some time and strong indicators will be pointing in this direction, but the final test of 'willing workers' provides the seal.

I have always worked on the principle that we should ask those who live in the locality or nearby to be the ones committed to the proposed new work. If we are to 'work out' our faith on the doorstep it seems the right assumption to make. However, not all those living locally will necessarily be the right people and, to provide the best mix of gifts, you may have to draw on others who live miles away. I usually follow this procedure:

1 CALL TOGETHER THOSE WHO LIVE IN THE AREA AND NEARBY

Make this meeting a high priority. Invite people personally by letter, rather than simply using a church notice. The significance of the new work needs to be highlighted.

As the idea of planting in their area has been in the church mind for some time local people have begun to get used to the notion that they may be part of it. Indeed, some of them may have been instrumental in focusing on their patch initially. Others will be attending the meeting apprehensively, and feeling some pressure from the leadership and their friends to get involved.

When you draw this group together they must be free to respond to God and not to pressure. The leaders must feel this themselves and not just say it, otherwise those who don't wish to take part will be left with a sense of condemnation. They will feel, 'I am not doing what the leadership want me to do.' Leaders' advice is to be considered, but it should acknowledge the importance of members arriving at their own conclusions in a spirit of peace.

2 CONTENT OF THE MEETING

Why are we planting this congregation?

The new congregation is *part* of the mission of the church. The whole church is on a mission all the time, not only now through church planting. You will need to highlight this point because some church members will be convinced that you believe that church planting is the only way, rather than a way.

The church is extending and focusing its ministry on a particular part of its parish or wider community. This is incarnational. Just as Jesus became man so that we can understand what God is like, we are 'causing the Word to be made flesh' through our compassion and witness.

Produce a map which outlines the extent of the work. This is done best by using an overhead projector so everyone can see clearly. Make it clear that we are aiming to share the Gospel with the people who live in this geographical area. Most of them never attend church and they are to be our responsibility over the next *few years*. Emphasize this long-term aspect of the work.

It is not easy

I begin by saying, 'There is one thing that is hard to achieve and another that is relatively easy. It is hard to achieve a large harvest of conversions, but it is reasonably easy to give opportunity to develop people's gifts.' Planting a congregation immediately provides so many new jobs: worship, children's work, administration, visitors and so on. Folk who have not excelled or have felt superfluous in the mother church come into their own. I have witnessed this on several occasions.

But what about the Kingdom business of conversions? This is the heart of what we are doing, but they don't come easily. I am speaking here of people changing kingdoms, moving from darkness to light. Conversion is the most radical experience that happens to anyone. It leads to God having freedom to transform from the inside.

Why is this hard? Firstly, Satan does not let his children go without a fight. He is a past master at snatching the Gospel from their ears (Mark 4), keeping them away from keen Christians, and using creative temptations to hold them in spiritual bondage.

Secondly, we have much to learn about identifying with the average unchurched person and don't realize how far they are from our type of Christian worship service and church culture. Putting the sign outside the new plant and delivering an attractive leaflet is totally insufficient to encourage them to cross the threshold.

Thirdly, our credibility in a community is often at a low ebb. The stark truth is we are unnoticed or uninteresting. Just as we may be unaware of the body-building club that meets on a Monday night at the leisure centre, lively Christians praising their hearts out in the local secondary school may be equally passed over.

Fourthly, and most importantly, the number of deep friendships that the average Christian has with unbelievers is either small or non-existent. This implies that our harvest is necessarily small.

Unity

One should emphasize three further aspects: prayer, evangelism and unity. At this stage, a word about unity.

It doesn't follow that unity comes naturally or easily, it requires effort. If those who are planting have a healthy love for God and for one another, have the purpose of the work clearly in focus, and desire to maintain the unity of the Spirit, fruit will follow in its wake. We are often too concerned with structures and giftedness, whereas God continues to highlight the importance of good relationships and unity. Where brothers and sisters live together in unity, God commands the blessing (Psalm 133).

Cover the following questions

• *Who will lead it?*

This is especially significant if the planting church enjoys strong leadership with a clear teaching ministry. Members are reluctant to lose out. Explain that the leader is absolutely key to the success of the work. Sow the seed at this point that it is not an ego trip for those not finding 'leadership recognition' in the church as a whole. Such folk, having a high profile in the plant, can cause havoc (see Chapter 7).

Identify who the leader is to be (an elder, someone trained in the church, a person to be employed with the appropriate qualities). This reassures the members that the new church will have the right sort of foundation.

• *Where will we meet?*

Look for the best building early on. Extensive plans can be made only to find that there is no suitable building to hire. Schools can be expensive, but I have always found them to be the best. There are always enough classrooms for the children's or group work. Often a village hall is too small or does not have sufficient ancillary rooms.

Be adventurous. The best place may be a pub, night club, or the civic hall. You may have to pray in the building on each occasion it is hired because of what has been taking place during the week.

- *What about other local Christians?*

Inform the meeting what has been done in contacting local clergy and the reaction that there has been. There will be a right sensitivity expressed, and again reassurance will be needed that we are going ahead without harming the Body of Christ.

- *What sort of evangelism?*

Most folk will think that they will have to be 'happy door-to-door visitors'. Explain that this will be part of the work, but as many types of evangelism as possible are advocated. However, the requirement of making friends with and praying for the salvation of individuals is central.

- *Do I have to be part of it?*

The answer is 'No!' However, remind them to be responsible in the decision they are making. God does want them to serve in some capacity.

- *Can we invite people to the congregation who live outside the area?*

Yes, if these are your friends who don't attend another church. However, we are trying to put most of our energy into this particular geographical patch.

- *Will I still attend the housegroup with my friends?*

This can be the hardest part for some — losing contact with close friends who won't be part of the plant. Most congregational planting will change the existing housegroup structures. Actually, this is a good thing and opens up new challenges, but will require careful handling.

In our most recent congregation in Guildford the following questions were asked of the group a few months after they had started on a Sunday. I wanted to discover their reasons for being involved at the outset. Those involved should have a correct understanding of the purpose and a sense of calling to the work.

1 *What was helpful about the way the church plant was explained to you?*

'The approach of having informal evenings where people could come with questions. Also, that there would be a period of preparation mid-week before starting on a Sunday.'

'It was realistic.'

'The explanation was gradual and did not require an instant response.'

Conclusion: To be as clear as possible about what is expected of individuals is crucial in helping the most suitable people to respond.

2 *What helped you to make up your mind?*

'Being in the location/vicinity where the church was to be planted.'

'Being personally asked to join for the contribution I could make.'

'An exciting challenge.'

Conclusion: For a number it was the personal challenge of 'coming out of the woodwork', i.e. it was possible to hide in the larger church.

The fact is our commitment to preach the Gospel to all nations transcends every other one. Adapting to the changes and making the personal sacrifices are part and parcel of our decision to be involved. Explain that spiritually they have more to gain than lose. If this is handled with sensitivity, folk will be encouraged to enlarge their vision and embrace the new challenge.

• *How do I decide?*

Suggest these questions to think over:

3 *Did you have conviction that it was God's call/will for you?*

'I've always felt that God's pattern was a *local* church instead of commuting to church.'

'Yes.'

Conclusion: Most of the group answered affirmatively to this question, but in our culture there is a reluctance to be too categorical about God's will in personal terms. People prefer to speak in terms of the most practical next step or the circumstances pointing in a particular direction. If we are 'too heavy' about them *definitely knowing they are called to the work*, we may put off some good people. All the folk who initially served in the congregation were suitable, but not all felt they could say it was God's will.

4 *How would you describe the purpose of the plant as you understood it at the time?*

'To bring others in the locality to Christ.'

'To reach people locally with Christ's love in a relevant way.'

'Befriending our neighbours, outreach, not high-pressure or "hit-and-run job".'

Conclusion: Although the evangelistic purpose is central, it can be sidelined. So, creative and inspiring ways are needed to highlight it, both at the beginning and throughout.

a) Have you more than a general concern for people to become Christians?

b) Have you a desire to work locally?

c) Are there gifts that are not being used that you can usefully employ in this ministry?

d) Are you willing to give the commitment outlined above?

e) Is God giving you His peace?

f) Does common sense lead you to believe that it is both the right and practical thing for you to do?

Also, offer the counsel of those in leadership to help with their decisions.

- *Where do we go from here?*

One way forward is to send a letter asking them to make a decision about whether they are going to be part of the group. This is helpful because it encourages them to come to some decision even if it is not to be involved. And, for those who are going to take part, it encourages them to 'sign on the dotted line'. I believe that being reasonably formal about this gives the work the significance that it will need to be successful. We don't want people to simply slip into it, because they will need to look back to an actual commitment when the going gets tough.

When these names are agreed you can move to the next stage of beginning to gel them together. It will be obvious from the numbers whether they need to be supplemented from the wider church body.

PREPARING THE TEAM FOR ACTION

Great value is gained from spending a few months gelling the core congregation together: providing training, beginning to make contact with the community, and working out 'who is to do what'. The idea that we can simply appear on the scene one Sunday and think that this will make an impact falls far short of the reality.

GELLING THE GROUP

Knowing one another well and spending time in building up fellowship has always been an integral part of the church since apostolic times (Acts 2:42). Sharing our love and faith in Jesus Christ and having a mutual supportiveness in weakness and strength lays the best foundation. However, too many churches have fallen into the trap of 'fellowship–itis' which has left precious little time to serve the world around us. It is, therefore, necessary from the outset to place our fellowship time in the context of service and evangelism.

To meet fortnightly, rather than weekly, provides the pattern and does not crowd people's lives with too many extra meetings. This gives the message that we are freeing up time to get involved in the locality, or to invite friends to a meal. This sounds good in theory and plans may be suggested, like joining the tennis club, or getting involved in the PTA, or frequenting the local pub, but good intentions are not always followed through. If possible, a weekend away could be arranged, mainly to have fellowship and to get to know one another. This need not be too expensive. One of our groups used the garden of a friend in the Cotswolds to camp. Catering was shared and a good time was had by all.

My own conviction is that fellowship is deepened when it is put in the context of action and vision. Working on a project together unites Christians – without this we are merely going round in circles or stagnating. Part of fellowship is in studying scripture together and again this can be related to the overall purpose. Topics from the book of Acts are eminently suitable. The following subjects are relevant: life in the community, the role of the Holy Spirit, pioneering new fields, what is involved in conversion?, and facing conflicts caused by the Gospel.

It is impossible to have close fellowship with more than a few people, and at some point smaller groupings within the larger one need to be provided. However, in these early days the group needs to gell as a whole and feel that they are a team together.

TRAINING

As well as formal training there is no substitute for on-the-job training. Nothing is more certain to drive us to our knees and dependence on God than getting involved with evangelistic activity. In some churches teaching is given, but members are not always provided with the opportunity or challenge to respond in practical ways. There is often a reluctance in leadership to ask members to take action in ways that they will find spiritually difficult. Until this changes we are going to make little progress.

In many other churches little training is taking place. We easily confuse teaching and training. Giving biblical teaching and principles on different subjects without opportunity to 'work it into our hearts and minds and then work it out in society' is inadequate teaching. So what sort of training should there be for the core group of church planters?

1 *Being part of a church committed to planting*

The group who are being sent out need to feel that they belong to a church who share a similar vision (see Chapter 7). A work will be birthed well if the church as a whole, and not just a section of the church who want to plant, know that they are committed to church planting. We know the expression about something being 'caught as well as taught'. There will be both security and encouragement for the planting group if they know and feel that what they are doing is in line with the church's overall ministry.

2 *A biblical understanding*

The Acts of the Apostles describes how Church growth took place through planting churches wherever the Gospel was preached. It is the biblical pattern, and evangelism without church planting would not have been contemplated. So a commitment to the principle will need to be in the core group's hearts.

Also, teaching the doctrine of the Church: The plant will necessarily have to have a strongly evangelistic thrust, but we are planting Church. Therefore, aspects of worship, discipleship, family, etc. will in time find their place.

3 *Loving relationships*

We are not planting a group of separate individuals, but folk who are learning to love one another and grow as a team. We cannot overlook the power of Jesus' prophecy: 'They will know you are my disciples, by the way that you love one another' (John 13:35). In the months before they begin on a Sunday, loving relationships are to be encouraged.

How is this done? As well as teaching scripture, provide opportunity for people to pray for one another. This releases the love of God, and the Holy Spirit knits people together. Also, organize social events and exercises that will open people up to one another.

The fact that they are united in such a significant task will help greatly in giving a sense of oneness. When folk join this congregation they will be more likely to stay if they experience a 'warm place'. I am always challenged by 1 John 4:12 which tells us that no one has seen God at any time; but as we love one another, He is seen in us.

4 *It's hard work*

They will face inevitable discouragements. They recognized at the outset that it would be hard work, but without being 'heavy-handed' remind them of this from time to time. Jesus continued to the end because He knew the magnitude of the task from the beginning.

The next chapter is devoted to the crucial elements of prayer and evangelism. But we can see from the above that developing biblical thinking and Christian character is the foundation on which prayer and evangelism are built.

MAKING CONTACT WITH THE COMMUNITY

It was agreed in our latest plant that as well as giving time to friendship we would use home events and visitation. Those who lived in the village were encouraged to hold a barbecue or the like and to invite their immediate neighbours. The point of the exercise was purely friendship, with no Gospel 'sting in the tail'. Often folk know very little about their neighbours and Christians can offer a service of bringing people together. These were very successful events but, of course, should not remain 'one-offs'. Christmas also affords an ideal opportunity to use our homes, to sing a few carols and provide refreshments.

We visited the 1,200 houses in our area but preceded the visit with a letter.

The letter was brief enough to read and gave information. It was genuinely interested in what the community felt. It offered Christian literature to those who wanted it. Later, a great many people were out so a card was left to explain why a personal visit would not be made.

We were encouraged in the following ways:

In recent months the Guildford Baptist Church (Millmead Centre) have been preparing to establish a congregation in Onslow Village. There are a number from the church who live in this community and the church leadership believe that there is need to provide a worship centre locally.

We are writing to you to make you aware of our plans and also to ask some questions to help us. In the next few days one of the local congregation will be calling on you and we should be grateful if you could think about the following questions. If you do not have the time, we quite understand.

- It is hoped that a Sunday service will begin in October of this year in one of the schools in the village. If you don't already attend another church, would you be interested in having more information?
- Is there a need for a mid-week children's and/or youth club in the area?
- There is a growing interest in spiritual things. Would you be interested in receiving literature or a video about the Christian faith?

Thank you for reading this letter.

The Guildford Baptist Church Leaders

Fig. 1 *Letter used prior to door-to-door visitation in Onslow Village, Guildford*

Fig. 2 *Follow-up card used in door-to-door visitation in Onslow Village, Guildford*

A member from Guildford Baptist Church (Millmead Centre) called at your home today to discuss the letter that was delivered, but unfortunately there was no one in.

If you would like a visit, please contact us on:

575008 (daytime)
572745 (evenings)

- People were aware that we were coming. Sometimes, when you explain that you are following up the letter that they received a few days ago, you are greeted with, 'What letter?'
- A number of folk were ready to receive literature or watch the video (it was *Journey into Life*[1]).
- Forty people said they would like information about the congregation nearer the time.
- The need for some provision for young people was established.
- A few people made contact with us on the basis of receiving the card, which surprised us.
- We came across a handful of people who expressed an interest in attending.
- There is value in informing the community several months before that a congregation is going to start. It takes a long time for the fact to sink in and for them to begin to ever imagine themselves attending.

PUBLICITY BEFORE THE FIRST SERVICE

About three weeks before we began a leaflet was distributed. Prior to this every member of the congregation was given responsibility for a road or roads, which meant that delivering publicity wasn't the burden of a few.

- The cartoon on the front gave the impression of friendliness and family.
- There were not too many words.
- Topics were chosen that were relevant to the unbeliever.

We continued to deliver a similar leaflet every three months.

WHO IS TO DO WHAT?

The leader will need to form a small team around him with the sort of gifts outlined earlier. This group can begin to talk through who is to take responsibility for the different aspects of the work. The obvious needs like musicians, teachers, administrator will already be in place, but what about the more practical jobs? People will be needed to:

GUILDFORD BAPTIST CHURCH
Onslow Village Congregation

A new church will be starting on 4th October at Queen Eleanor's Middle School, and you are very welcome to join with us. The services will begin at 10.00 a.m. and will end at about 11.15 a.m. with coffee.

We belong to the Guildford Baptist Church (Millmead Centre) and want to provide a local congregation for those who have faith in Jesus Christ, and for others who are interested. We have tried to provide subjects that are relevant to most people.

We visited the houses in Onslow Village a few months ago and we have been encouraged by the interest from many. We recognize that some of you already have a commitment to another church and we are not wanting to draw you away.

The basic questions of life are often left unanswered, but we believe that knowing Jesus Christ provides the framework for addressing them.

If you would like to make contact before October, please ring: 575008 (daytime), 572745 (evening).

THERE WILL BE NO SERVICE ON THE FINAL SUNDAY OF EACH MONTH

Guildford Baptist Church
Onslow Village Congregation ...

During the service there will be something for every age group, and part of the time children will be catered for in their own group and créche. Could you let us know if you will be bringing children with you.

We will be taking themes in October and November from the early chapters of Genesis, and in December from the gospel of Matthew.

October
4 In the beginning God . . .
   How can we be sure God created?
   (Genesis 1)
11 Then there were two
   God still believes in marriage
   (Genesis 2)
18 It's your choice!
   What makes people do wrong?
   (Genesis 3)

November
1 Brotherly hate
   Why do people not get on with each other?
   (Genesis 4)

November
8 It rained and rained and rained
   Why was there a flood?
   (Genesis 6)
15 Back to the drawing board
   What is involved in making a spiritual start?
   (Genesis 8 and 9)
22 Moving in the right direction
   Learning lessons from one of the greatest?
   (Genesis 12)

December
6 Skeletons in the cupboard
   You will be surprised who is in the family tree of the Lord Jesus
   (Matthew 1)
13 Born of a virgin
   How can Jesus be both God and man?
   (Matthew 1)
20 A Christmas Celebration for all the family

Fig. 3 *Publicity used in Onslow Village, Guildford*

- Open and close the building if there is no caretaker.
- Bring the refreshments and prepare them. Check what facilities are in the building.
- Prepare the hall and classrooms. This job requires very reliable people because it is possible to grow weary in well-doing.
- Find a place to store the equipment: overhead projector, screen, PA, Bibles, song books, etc.
- Welcome at the door.
- Put up the sign advertising 'who you are'. Usually this needs to be done each week, as no permanent advertising is allowed.

Children

Children can be the main reason why a family won't get involved with a new congregation. In my experience, far more children are happier in a new/smaller plant than in the church they have left. This could be because far more thought, care and attention is given to 'getting it right'.

The children's leader requires the same qualities as anyone holding a similar position in a church. However, the ability to be adaptable to a different environment, and flexible in ordering the programme differently are recommended. As the children's programme will be smaller than the one that they have left, there is freedom for family involvement across the age groups and a more informal approach.

WHAT DO YOU CALL YOURSELVES?

A name can be chosen that means a lot to members of the congregation but nothing to those who we are intending to reach. If the mother church has credibility in an area then link the name of the congregation to it. There is no point in starting from scratch in a community. There is enough suspicion of new cults and, with the wrong name, the world may think that your new congregation is in the same category. Elim's *Kensington Temple's Manual for Church Planters*[2] says, 'In choosing a name we need to consider the following:

- The culture of the people we are trying to reach and their local identity.
- The impression the name is going to make on the local people.
- Would the unchurched be comfortable coming to a church with a name like that?
- Will the name give the impression that the church is part of "mainstream" Christianity or possibly a cult?

'What *not* to call your church:

- Pentecostal Tabernacle of Steadfast Love
- Zoe Temple of the First Born
- Barakah Fellowship
- This Little Light of Mine Fellowship of the Narrow Way
- Anything that remotely resembles any of the above!'

ONE FINAL THOUGHT – A TRIAL RUN FIRST

It would be chaotic to arrive at the venue on the first morning and not know how to arrange the chairs, where the plugs are, and where the musicians are to be situated. All this can be ironed out by having a dry run during mid-week. It will give the core group confidence as well as an idea of what it will feel like.

four

PRAYER AND EVANGELISM

TWO VITAL INGREDIENTS

Prayer and relevant evangelism are the indispensable elements that lie at the heart of church planting. They are often given high priority in the initial discussions and early days, but are usually the first to be neglected. Why is this? All of us know that without huge discipline prayer will give place to 'other things'. Our time soon gets filled. It doesn't take very long for a church to start looking inward, often for legitimate reasons, losing the stimulus of all that might be termed evangelistic.

Satan attempts to undermine the spiritual effectiveness of the church by mounting his assaults against these two vital elements. My greatest spiritual pressure from Satan's kingdom is experienced when I put emphasis on prayer and motivating the church evangelistically. I sense that he does this to dissuade me from continuing to give a strong lead. However, 'The devil trembles when he sees the weakest saint upon his knees.' This is true, and when we add a determination to reach out to unbelievers we become an even greater concern to him.

So a commitment to prayer and evangelism will not come easily and will open us to severe spiritual attack from the evil one. From the outset they should be built into the foundation of the church life so that they will not easily be set aside.

THE IMPORTANCE OF PRAYER IN THE FIRST PLANTING CHURCH

The Acts of the Apostles is history but is full of principles for dynamic church life. It describes the exciting development of the Church in the first thirty years. There were ten different aspects of prayer which enabled the early believers to continue to fulfil the commission in the midst of human, religious, worldly and demonic pressures. What have we to learn from them?

1 The early disciples 'joined together constantly in prayer' in the days leading up to Pentecost (Acts 1:14). They knew that it was only in the power of the Holy Spirit that the great commission would be fulfilled. They did not only wait in Jerusalem, but waited with **constant** prayer. They could have no clear idea at that stage how it would be answered in detail, but had utter conviction that this was the method.

2 **Worship** and **praise** in the Holy Spirit had extremely powerful effects on the visitors to Jerusalem in Acts 2. 'The Jews and converts to Judaism from the Diaspora heard the disciples declaring the wonders of God in their own languages.' Although a one-off and therefore unique event, the place of worship and strong praise of God in the midst of not-yet believers will bear its own fruit. It was the Spirit-empowered relevant words that gripped them and caused them to say, 'What must we do to be saved?' (Acts 2:37)

3 The apostles **founded** the emerging Church on prayer. Alongside teaching, fellowship and breaking of bread, intimate contact with the Father was central. The early Christians were taught to be devoted to these foundational aspects (Acts 2:42). The Church throughout the centuries has been challenged by this verse and the ones that follow, as a model for close fellowship and healthy evangelism. 'They had everything in common . . . and the Lord added to their number daily those who were being saved.' (Acts 2:44, 47)

4 It was **regular** prayer that met with reward. Peter and John were merely following their normal practice of going to the temple at the hour of prayer when a significant healing took place (Acts 3:1–10). Regular prayer is more often associated with discipline than with delight. Every time believers regularly meet together to pray we are opening ourselves to God's opportunities.

5 The early Church teaches us to pray in **desperate** situations. In Acts 4 Peter and John are threatened with punishment if they continued to speak and teach in the name of Jesus. Then in Acts 12 James is murdered and Peter imprisoned. It is in these desperate times that desperate prayer is called for. Too often we retreat when the authorities put up obstacles. But we too need to pray 'Sovereign Lord' and experience the shaking of the Holy Spirit and the angelic messengers setting our captives free.

6 In any growing church busyness is almost inevitable. In every church, large or small, busy or not, prayer must be the **priority**. The apostles found themselves busy with work that was not God's best for them. A time of reassessment was required. The matter was resolved by intelligent delegation and a return to their first calling. 'We must give ourselves to prayer and the ministry of the word.' (Acts 6:4) Over the years God has spoken to me several times through this verse to give to prayer the priority it demands. This is the way the Kingdom works and must challenge our busy, and sometimes unfruitful, lives.

7 God **spoke** whilst the believers prayed. Ananias is famous because he heard God's voice in a vision. He was told, 'Go to the house of Judas on Straight Street and ask for a man from Tarsus named Saul . . . In a vision he has seen a man named Ananias come and place his hands on him to restore his sight.' (Acts 9:11–12) A similar thing happened to the apostle Peter and Cornelius. Both had a vision. Cornelius, a Roman centurion at Caesarea, and later Peter at Joppa (Acts 10–11).

The results of these two events were crucial to the furtherance of the early Church. The apostle Paul received encouragement and nurture, and was being prepared for his ministry to the Gentiles. Peter heard God's voice so deeply that he needed to open his heart to the Gentiles because this was the heart of God's will for him. This essential element of receiving revelation remains key to God continuing to reach 'those who are near and far off'.

8 Prayer and fasting for **right decisions**. God works through people. The Church functions best when the right people are doing the right jobs. In Acts 13 we witness a crucial prayer meeting. Prophets and teachers had been worshipping the Lord and fasting, and then the Holy Spirit said, 'Set apart Barnabas and Saul for the work to which I have called them.' (Acts 13:2) I'm sure that the church in Antioch would have had other plans for these two, but special fasting led to the making of right decisions. No one can deny the huge contribution that these men made in their missionary journeys.

Right decision-making about people is also seen when the planted churches are provided with spiritual oversight. 'Paul and Barnabas appointed elders for them in each church and, with prayer and fasting, committed them to the Lord, in whom they had put their trust.' (Acts 14:23) Some of the most important decisions that we have to make are about people, and in order to get it right special prayer is essential.

9 When there is nowhere else to turn, prayer expresses our **confidence in God**. Paul and Silas were imprisoned at Philippi after being severely flogged. Such is their confidence in God that we read, 'About midnight Paul and Silas were praying and singing hymns to God, and the other prisoners were listening to them.' (Acts 16:25) This is the time of the earthquake, when the jailor's family were converted and the apostles freed, leaving the authorities embarrassed.

10 Prayer will **open and close doors**. Paul 'had been kept by the Holy Spirit' from preaching the word in the province of Asia. They tried to enter Bithynia but 'the Spirit of Jesus would not allow them'. It is at this point that Paul receives his vision of the Macedonian who says, 'Come over and help us.' (Acts 16:6–10)

Why not Asia and Bithynia, and why Macedonia? Weren't all of them in need of Christ? We see the place of God's strategy and timing made clear to Paul through sensitivity to the Holy Spirit. In our increasingly cosmopolitan society, we need equal responsiveness to God's leading through prayer and vision to reach each segment of society.

This is a Spirit-filled catalogue of the early believers being in close touch with God through different aspects of prayer. It resulted in churches being planted and established from Jerusalem to Rome.

WHAT SORT OF PRAYER?

What are the practical ways in which a church planting congregation can employ prayer? All that has been said about the early Church are good principles, but what about the 'how'?

PRAYER WALKING

A few years ago prayer walking was thought to be strange, even 'over the top'. However, it has now been accepted in many more circles as a powerful tool of evangelism. Scripture highlights a few individuals who might have been the forerunners of this activity. Joshua was told that every place where he set his foot would be given to him by the Lord (Joshua 1:3). And I suppose the thirteen times round the city of Jericho was the original prayer walk. Nehemiah walked Jerusalem by night, weighing up how the rebuilding of the temple should take place (Nehemiah 3).

What is happening when you go out walking? You are not only looking with natural eyes, but also with the eyes of the Spirit. You are asking to see things as God sees them, and feel them as He feels. You are taking note of significant places, schools, council offices, public houses, etc. Praying for people and places outside is a very different experience to praying in the church prayer meeting. This type of prayer is not spoken aloud nor is it trying to draw attention to the pray-ers. The purpose is to fill your road and community with prayer. Those folk who walk past you will have no idea what you are doing. Working as a couple or threesome is probably the most encouraging. As you walk (with your eyes open) you talk to the Lord. The people who see you probably think you are sharing in a conversation together.

At the outset of a congregational plant, walking the roads is standard practice. The Anglicans used to have a yearly ceremony where they 'beat the bounds'. The local Christians walked around the parish proclaiming God's rule and commanding the evil spirits to leave. Those involved in the new church can encircle the geographical boundaries of the new plant in groups of two, possibly changing partners from time to time.

On the first occasion that I did this my friend found himself praying against crime and drugs. He didn't know it, but the Spirit had led him to pray accurately concerning a house on that road. Churches in Reading have been using prayer walking for several years. On one particular estate, known for its high crime rate, a church has been successfully planted and the crime rate has reduced by 40 per cent. This is credited to the consistent prayer walking, coupled with a church planting project. John Dawson gives many specific stories of the effect of this approach in his book, *Taking Our Cities for God*.[1]

A PRAYER MISSION

We had a prayer mission for one of our new congregations. Members of our church, who were not involved in the church plant themselves, were asked to give one hour of their time over a three-day period. We asked them to do three things:

- to follow a particular route so all the roads in the area were covered;
- to pray specifically for homes where we had sensed there was an interest (through earlier door-to-door visiting);
- to listen to the Lord.

If there was a spiritual power that was opposing us in that community we wanted divine guidance about it and any divine intelligence about individuals. As most of the people who took part had no previous experience of prayer walking, we were very encouraged by the results. Inevitably, a number of our walkers spoke in general terms, because it takes time to develop more accurate 'listening to the Lord'. Quite a lot of individual comments were made which were not corroborated. This doesn't mean they were inaccurate, but we have felt it wise not to accept everything that was shared. The more specific information was as follows:

- Concerning certain houses, the same point was made by different people. There was no consultation between them and this made it doubly exciting. Some of the houses on the routes had been identified, but our prayer walkers gave information about other individual houses that weren't on their list. When this was reported back to the group, a sense of awe came over us. God was informing us of how to care and pray for people.

Some might feel that this kind of prayer is intrusive, but this is not the purpose. The prayer mission was held in order to express our love and concern for the community, and to ask God's guidance for the health and healing of individuals. It would appear that the Lord is ready to grant this sort of information.

- On a couple of roads a feeling of darkness and oppression was felt, only to be followed by a sense of light when the walkers moved on to another road. And on two other roads, a sense of sadness and emptiness was experienced.

- On one road two people mentioned that they were stirred to pray in tongues and there was a sense that 'something needed to be broken' in that particular community.

I'm sure that those who took part have increased their prayer concern for this area of Guildford through their involvement in the mission. I believe it had been a rewarding and very helpful experiment, and so the group has been asked to repeat the exercise in a few months' time.

WARFARE PRAYING

Warfare praying is still a very controversial subject and evangelical Christians are having to agree to differ over what it entails. I am persuaded that battling prayer against the principalities and powers is required if we want to witness a large harvest of new Christians. The rationale behind this is that Satan is a strategist. We are not wrestling against flesh and blood, but different levels of evil authorities which have controlling power in our villages, towns and cities.

This is a huge subject and cannot adequately be covered in this section. However, there are three main views held concerning spiritual warfare (according to Brenda Marks (née Robson) a team associate of Guildford Community Church). There is truth in each of them and local churches will vary as to which of them receives most emphasis.

View one

There is a mass or group of fallen angels all having become evil,
probably of varying orders, but who have all maintained their
power and rank. They all operate on the earth and they are the
rulers of this present age, this current darkness. Their background
is in this world. Some have their sphere of operations on a personal
level with individuals, whilst others are principalities and powers
or spiritual forces of evil. These are all demonic spirits ruling over
a geographic location or a people. They are able to bind the minds
of unbelievers throughout the world.

The emphasis here is on discernment, deliverance, and binding
and loosing prayer. Main scriptures: Matthew 16:19; 2 Corinthians
10:3–5; Ephesians 6:10–18; Isaiah 14:12–15; Daniel 10:2–11:1;
Psalm 149:6–9.

View two

Demons can either be personal or geographical but, except in
personal exorcism, the powers of darkness are pushed back by
preaching the Gospel and doing the works of Jesus in the
community. Thus, the concentration is on the works of Jesus
rather than the works of Satan.

The emphasis here is on personal deliverance and doing the
works of Jesus. Main scriptures: Ephesians 3:10; Acts 19; Matthew
12:25–29.

View three

This belief is that the structures of society are created by God but
can become demonized by idolatry and thus serve the purposes
of Satan rather than God. Recognition of this invisible power, in
whatever form whether in a person or groups, is by its
manifestation of death in all its forms rather than by definition.
To deal with evil spirits' dominion over men and women is the
work of the Church, though not in offensive combat but in
demonstration of humility and sacrifice, the supreme example of
which is Jesus on the cross. Only in this way will injustice be dealt
with and true justice prevail.

The emphasis here is on the pursuit of justice through humility and sacrifice. Main scriptures: Galatians 4:8; 1 Corinthians 2:6.

How is this done?

A large part of warfare prayer is to be actively praying for the coming of the Kingdom of God against the powers of evil. Many would argue that the praise marches which fill towns and cities with the name of Jesus have made significant differences to the controlling powers of a town. Both are committed to taking prayer into the heart of the community.

Teaching on strategic spiritual warfare was given in Guildford. About 200 Christians from many different churches were addressed. After the sixth teaching and prayer session it was agreed that the group should meet on a monthly basis. They had already formed themselves into groups, according to the different areas of Guildford in which they lived as well as further afield. It seems that giving Christians specific responsibility for their locality heightens their commitment. The groups have been researching local history to uncover which powers are hindering the work of the Gospel. This has resulted in covering each segment of the Guildford district with concentrated prayer in order to bring in the Kingdom of God.

An active proclamation of the Gospel needs to accompany the warfare prayer, as well as getting involved with people and the community in order to demonstrate the love and power of God in Jesus. This sort of action is relatively new and we must wait to see the extent of its effect. However, it appears from research in other countries, particularly Argentina, that the fruit of it is incalculable.

ALL TYPES

Christians can be mobilized to enter into special times of prayer even if they struggle with the regular, disciplined variety. To call the occasional day of fasting, at the beginning of a new season or in relation to times of visiting or special events, brings its own rewards. We need creativity. So many prayer meetings have become staid and predictable. It is the same faithful few who attend. Of course God will be gracious in answering, and I am not despising faithfulness. We can, however, help ourselves enormously by having a more flexible structure. It provides opportunity for new groups to start and others to begin to attend an existing group.

After the first few years at West Bridgford I suggested that we stop the 7 a.m. prayer meeting. About ten of us had met for about three years each Wednesday morning. It had been a very effective time of prayer and I attribute much of the early development of the church to it. However, the time came to open out new possibilities for the church as a whole, and so a different structure was suggested. A couple of members in the group thought it a retrograde step, because they thought it meant giving up prayer. However, I believe this approach helps a church and keeps our praying fresh.

Usually when you have special times of prayer someone will suggest that it should continue on a regular basis. We need to capitalize on the enthusiasm, but give it a shape that can be reviewed after a period of time. This also helps people to know the extent of the commitment at the outset.

EVANGELISM

One of the lecturers at Cliff College, where I was a student, kept a record of all the different types of evangelism that he had come across. During one of the lectures we were given a list of about a hundred different methods. If he were still lecturing it would be twice, if not three times, as long now.

It is more important for a church to have an evangelistic orientation rather than the occasional event. If a group have evangelism in their attitudes, and near to the surface of their minds, events will automatically follow.

HOW IS EVANGELISM DEVELOPED WITHIN THE CHURCH?

Chris and Sue Scupham began to lead the Baptist church in Chadwell Heath. The church had about twenty to twenty-five active members at the time and was willing to change. Over the next six years the church grew considerably through conversions. The things that were tried there illustrate the possibilities for any church.

- *Older people*

  The church only had a few older people. Coffee mornings and afternoons were tried to gather folk together in homes, but unsuccessfully. A demographic survey revealed that OAPs were increasing in the community.

  Would a luncheon club work? By making the church hall attractive and offering lunch at cost price with waitress service, numbers of elderly folk began to come. Information about the church was available at the tables, as well as friendship and genuine interest shown in them. A fellowship group started after the meal and non-church people stayed for it. This led to some of these folk attending church.

- *Reaching young people*

  There were only a couple of teenagers in the church. The traditional youth club was not working. With the help of an Oasis team, and also allowing the young people to set the agenda, an informal non-alcoholic cocktail bar was introduced. Part of the church hall was used and suitably decorated. Again, it led to relationships being established, church attendance, and commitments to Christ.

- *Ladies' group*

  For about two years an event for women took place monthly in the church. It did not set out to have meetings centred on the Christian message, although occasionally did so. A speaker was invited and subjects like Dr Barnardo's, first aid in the home, colour coding, entertaining under-fives, were covered. Meeting together and discussing life issues established friends and provided a platform for sharing Jesus Christ more personally.

- *Reaching married couples*

  An event was arranged every couple of months to which couples could be invited. Again, these were designed to relate to people in a social context in order to demonstrate that Christians were not abnormal. (Unfortunately many of us are considered strange or odd by those outside the church.) So what sort of events? 1950s/1960s parties, reflecting the music played and clothes worn; quiz nights; a dinner with a speaker; barn dances; and fish and chip suppers.

- *Pantomime*

  The church wrote a pantomime to present around Christmas time. The Christian message can quite easily be presented through such an approach. Pantomimes are full of 'goodies' and 'baddies'. In the first year 350 people attended, the following year 500 came to see the presentation. In a church of about 120 this stretched resources but was yet another tool for contacting the community.

The church also had seasons of more overt evangelism, like door-to-door knocking and using *Good News Down the Street*[2], a short Bible study course for those enquiring. The Scuphams tried not to overload the members with too great an evangelistic commitment, recognizing that they would grow tired. Chris and Sue moved on from Chadwell Heath after six years, when the attendance was around 100/120 on a Sunday morning, and have left a church who are more naturally evangelistic.

The work of the above church is illustrative of what can take place in a newly planted church, which may start with a similar number. They did have the advantage of a building, which must not be overlooked. However, it was the desire to reach people that was the underlying motivation. Those planting a church without their own building will have to be more resourceful, but their commitments to make friendships and proclaim the truths of the Gospel will prove equally effective.

SEEKER–FRIENDLY SERVICES

Unfortunately a lot of what happens in our worship services is unintelligible to the average unchurched person. In one sense we should not be too worried about this because our experience of Christ is through the working of the Holy Spirit. We only understand the Gospel through a revelation from God and not intellect. As Paul says, 'The man without the Spirit does not accept the things that come from the Spirit of God, for they are foolishness to him, and he cannot understand them, because they are spiritually discerned.' (1 Corinthians 2:14)

What happens in church must be real. We should talk to God in language that everyone understands and explain Christian truth as simply as possible. Those who join us who are not used to church should feel that they are welcome, sense the peace of God amongst us, and understand the words even if they haven't experienced them. When born again, they will see the Kingdom of God (John 3:3).

Bill Hybels had a vision of creating a church for the unchurched. So, in the Willow Creek Community Church in Chicago the Christians meet during the week for their worship and teaching. Sunday is reserved for the unchurched, where a service is held with which they will be able to identify in every detail. Martin Robinson describes this church in detail[3] and many from this country were able to attend a conference addressed by Bill Hybels. This has led to a number of churches rethinking their Sunday to make their services more seeker-friendly.

INGREDIENTS OF A SEEKER—FRIENDLY SERVICE

At Millmead we have held a few seeker—friendly services on Sunday mornings. This has value, but to hold them on a more regular basis would be more effective and sustain continuity with the unchurched who have been attending. Here is an example of one such service.

Announcements

At the beginning we made it clear that we were holding a different type of service, where the emphasis was on presentation rather than personal involvement in worship. Our visitors were welcomed and informed of the finishing time. We had planned the service to end after one hour and fifteen minutes, which coincided with

Chris Stoddard of Southcourt Baptist Church, Aylesbury attended the Willow Creek Conference in this country and subsequently followed it up with a visit to Willow Creek itself. For several years he had been challenged that the church should be trying to find ways to reach the unchurched. Southcourt was growing and open to experiment with a different type of service which would meet the needs of unbelievers.

Would it be monthly or weekly? It was agreed that it must take place each week, for continuity purposes. Initially three were planned. These were considered to be a success and a further decision was taken to run from January to Easter, each Sunday evening. In March a decision needed to be made about what was to happen after Easter. The matter was fully discussed within the church and a vote taken of those in favour of continuing indefinitely. As this meant a complete change of evening worship for the foreseeable future it required support from the members. Over 90 per cent voted in favour of continuing to use their evening worship to reach the unchurched.

Chris worked with about fifty of the church members and was encouraged by the talent that emerged. They have used the different media employed by Willow Creek, with each service following only one theme and lasting no longer than an hour. The same subject is usually covered over a three-week period – such

our children's programme. Also at this point an offering was announced, which would be taken during the first hymn. Our visitors were given freedom not to contribute. We announced the theme: 'Is Jesus really the only way to God?' (See Appendix B for original material used during this service.)

Hymns and songs

Only four hymns/songs were used and we were reasonably sure that our visitors would be familiar with them ('Shine Jesus Shine', 'Majesty', 'Amazing Grace' and 'Man of Sorrows').

Children

We decided to include the children for the first fifteen minutes and address them in line with the overall theme of the service. A dramatic sketch used on this occasion, called *Ticket to Heaven*, was performed with the help of puppets.

topics as health, wealth and happiness; why believe in God?; why believe in the Bible?'; love is . . .; keeping up appearances. Afterwards a buffet meal is available, where conversations take place naturally. A bulletin is given to each person, with information about the church and who to contact if they wish to talk further.

The move to adopt this sort of evening service caused the church to rethink their mission statement. Like Willow Creek, they wanted a simple sentence which each member could both know and own. They agreed on 'Bringing people to Jesus Christ and growing up in Him.' This can be further abbreviated to *going* and *growing*.

Who comes and why? They decided to advertise by word of mouth and personal invitation, so the folk who have come have been family, friends and work colleagues. This leads to the unchurched themselves inviting their friends. They appreciate the non-threatening aspect of the service and can come and observe without commitment, enjoying great variety.

In the first few weeks about ten people made commitments, but this average has not been maintained. Chris is not concerned about this because, according to Willow Creek, it takes on average eight to twelve months before a person makes a commitment to Christ. So the church is committed to a long-term, and therefore, more substantial work.

Use of tape-recorded material

After the children left, three minutes of a tape recording by Steve Chalke were played.[4] This highlighted that, however sincere we might be about what we believe, we can be sincerely wrong.

More drama

Another church member wrote a sketch illustrating the uniqueness of Jesus Christ as the only one who can lead us to God. It lasted six minutes, was light-hearted and helped to relax the congregation, but was very clear in its message.

Solo

Two Millmead members, who have written lyrics and music for many Christian and secular songs, also took part. I asked them to write a new song to fit our theme. One has an excellent singing voice and the other, who is a professional musician, prepared the backing tape to accompany her. This item was particularly well received as the words were clearly audible and the style contemporary.

The reading

John 14:1–11 was chosen as a background to the service theme. Two church members, who are particularly gifted in dramatic reading, shared this Bible passage.

The message

The theme was then addressed for twenty minutes. Alongside the preaching, illustrations appeared on a screen using an overhead projector. I have discovered that the message is understood and remembered more easily if visual aids are used to back up the spoken word.

   After the message I explained that a summary of the talk was available for visitors to take away with them. I made it clear that stewards would be at the exits and they could be asked for one of these leaflets. I also explained that a special prayer had been prepared at the end of the leaflet, if any of our visitors would like to make use of it personally. I have done this on each occasion and have found that visitors are willing to ask for them. (See Appendix B for the leaflet.)

GOING TO THE PEOPLE

Friendship-building and inviting people to services or events are one type of evangelism. However, we need to find ways of reaching the vast majority who are not going to come onto our territory. Our most fruitful evangelism will be amongst those who know us and who, through our witness, will begin to believe in and receive Jesus Christ. We return to the word 'go' again. We have to find ways of going to the people. Ultimately it will only be the compassion of Jesus and obedience to His word that will change us from people who say 'come' to those who are willing to 'go'.

Enabling a church to develop an evangelistic heart

Like a good many churches, Millmead is evangelical but not very evangelistic. This revealed itself in how few people were brought to special services which were appropriate for unbelievers. The sad fact is that so many Christians do not have non-Christian friends to bring to church. This needed to be faced squarely.

We coined a phrase in the church: outward and Kingdom and not only inward and Church. This simply meant that we needed to add to our very good internal church-life programme another dimension. I organized a six-month programme to highlight our needs to grow in evangelism and to begin to develop relationships with unbelieving friends. This coincided with a new emphasis within housegroups to become aware of the communities in which they met. Once a month we invited a speaker to open out an evangelistic theme and then asked the church to work this out practically within their smaller groups.

I hoped this would result in a growing number of people who would become part of Millmead's fringe. Not everyone has taken this on board by any means, but some have taken it to heart, making a deeper commitment to live out their faith within a work context. This is eminently sensible because it is the place where they spend most of their time.

The elders and I are committed to leading the fellowship into the community, and one natural consequence of this is the amount of quality time we give to those who are not yet Christians. A church has to work at this for a period of months, if not years, because there will be so many other legitimate demands on the time of its people. I believe that the Spirit is saying to the churches that we have concentrated on our teaching and good fellowship quite enough, and it is now time for us to express our love and witness to the world.

VISITING

Most of us have to overcome the hurdle of thinking that we won't be welcome on our local doorsteps. What are the guidelines?

Be friendly

As people open the door they are more likely to listen to what you have to say if you have a genuine smile and interest in them. This is likely to be a very brief encounter, with very little time to make contact. Ask the Lord to relax you and to convey God's love through you.

Explain clearly where you are from

There is so much suspicion about unusual religious movements that they will be reassured to know which church you are from. Of course, at this point the mention of the word 'church' may close the conversation. If this is the case, continue to be friendly and bid them farewell. God can speak through our attitudes.

If we expect all the people to be warm and interested in what we have to say we are going to be disappointed. We should ask God for genuine love and compassion for people and then their reaction will not alter our attitude to them.

Why are you visiting?

State clearly the reason for calling. It might be one of the following:

- You are hoping to start a new congregation in the next few months and wanted to know if they would like information.
- You are a new church in the area and are making yourselves known to the community.
- You have begun a new church in this locality and wondered if they could spare a couple of minutes whilst you explain why the Christian faith is important to you.
- You want to be helpful in the community and wondered if there is anything the church can do for them. The Ichthus Fellowship have used this approach very successfully through their Jesus Action programme. You need to be sure that you can provide the help before you make such an offer.

If visiting at Easter, a relevant question could be asked. I once went out with a group on Good Friday and asked the question, 'Do you know why Jesus Christ died on the cross?' I observed that people were not offended by the question, but again, the right approach is important.

How to pitch the level – from merely making yourself known to asking evangelical questions – will depend on the confidence of the visitor and the extent to which prayer has prepared the community. Some have found questionnaires very successful. These should be used with integrity and not merely as a tool to speak about Christ. Wanting to know people's opinions is a first step in reaching them for Christ.

Be flexible in how the conversation develops

If the person is willing to talk with you, allow them to set the agenda to a certain extent. Some people need to express their hurt over previous church experience. They will only listen to you if they have cleared this debris out of the way. Again, your reaction is important. Don't defend the church unnecessarily. If they are right in what they are saying, agree with them. However, you are there to commend the Body of Christ, not to pull down the reputation of another church.

Some conversations can become quite deep. If they feel they can trust you, personal needs will be shared and opportunities given to pray for them. Listen to the Holy Spirit and ask Him to guide you. What starts as a chance encounter can lead to the beginnings of a response to Jesus Christ.

Don't over-stay your welcome

Learn to tell the difference between genuine interest being shown and politeness. This isn't so hard these days because most people express their attitudes and feelings more easily. If conversation has developed, don't be afraid to ask if you are detaining them. This gives them freedom to end the conversation and close the door.

Have some literature

Even if the person doesn't want to talk you can ask if they would like to receive a piece of literature. Embarrassment or pressure of time means that some visits are very brief. But literature may be read when they have more time and they can think things through without pressure. The literature should be attractive and easy to assimilate. The availability of computer software means that visually interesting leaflets with local application can be produced.

FINDING WAYS TO GET INVOLVED

Gerald Coates tells the story of a group, from his own church in Cobham, who decided to clear a patch of waste ground. It belonged to no one in the community and the council felt no responsibility. A landscaping team were called together and one evening set to work on making it beautiful. The work eventually advertised itself, commending the church as committed to the community in practical ways.

There are plenty of ways to get involved in the local community. One lady I heard of recently stressed to her minister that she considered the Neighbourhood Watch Scheme her main ministry. She had given time to getting to know the neighbours in order to care for them. Some churches have members who are school governors in each of the schools in their community. Another church has encouraged members to stand as local councillors. The possibilities are many and various. We have spoken for so long about getting involved in the community in order to live, speak and influence for the name of Jesus. The extent of church growth will be proportionate to our commitment of 'going into all the world'.

five

DECIDING WHERE TO PLANT

BIBLICAL PRINCIPLES

What can be learned from the early Church about deciding where to plant? The plan of action is outlined by Jesus Christ in the first chapter of the Acts of the Apostles (1:8) — Jerusalem, Judea, Samaria and the ends of the earth. Hence, every church must begin locally but, at the same time, expect to be challenged with a world-wide vision. Jesus is merely restating the great commission in another way (Matthew 28:18–20). The emphasis in Matthew is on making disciples, whereas Acts stresses witnessing. Acts describes the beginning of the process, and Matthew the end result.

We can learn several principles from Acts, even though it records church planting in an international context rather than a local or regional one. Most importantly, the Holy Spirit is the main agent leading the whole operation. Alongside Him are individuals and the Church, involved in the strategic planning.

A SPIRIT-LED CHURCH

1 The apostles **used the opportunities** created by the Holy Spirit. Although they were expecting the Holy Spirit to come to them after the resurrection, God chose to delay the moment until Pentecost — one of their significant feasts. As a result of this Godly intervention, and the people's questions, 'Peter stood up and addressed the crowd', explaining the prophecy of Joel and preaching the Gospel (Acts 2).

When the lame man was healed on the way to the temple (3:1–10), the Spirit created another moment to speak, through the initiative of Peter and John. 'While the beggar held on to

Peter and John, all the people were astonished and came running to them in the place called Solomon's Colonnade. When Peter saw this, he said to them: "Men of Israel . . ." ' (3:11–12)

It was because Stephen was doing great wonders and miraculous signs among the people that he received such opposition. Falsely accused before the Sanhedrin and face shining like an angel, he is asked by the High Priest whether or not the charges are true. Again, the door is opened to present the Gospel, in the form of a sermon that led to his martyrdom (6:8–7:59).

2 **Persecution leads** to the **spread of the Gospel**. It was almost inevitable that the highly effective witness, together with the accompanying power of the Holy Spirit seen in Jerusalem, would lead to severe persecution of believers (8:1–3). Those persecuted spread out everywhere, not only witnessing, but establishing churches. 'Those who had been scattered preached the word wherever they went. Philip went down to a city in Samaria and proclaimed the Christ . . . There was great joy in that city.' (8:4–8).

'Now those who had been scattered by the persecution in connection with Stephen travelled as far as Phoenicia, Cyprus and Antioch, telling the message only to Jews. Some of them, however, men from Cyprus and Cyrene, went to Antioch and began to speak to Greeks also . . . The Lord's hand was with them, and a great number of people believed and turned to the Lord.' (11:19–21)

3 The Spirit is always **highlighting mission**. The plan is to get to the ends of the earth. Whenever the Holy Spirit is given freedom to speak, we find Him reminding the Church of its primary purpose. The Gospel travelled hundreds of miles from Jerusalem, but had much further to go yet. 'Whilst the leaders at Antioch were fasting and praying, the Holy Spirit said, "Set apart Barnabas and Saul for the work to which I have called them." ' (13:2) This was a worthy and sacrificial decision that led to the first of Paul's missionary journeys.

When Paul's friends tried to dissuade him from going to

Jerusalem he responded, 'And now compelled by the Spirit, I am going to Jerusalem, not knowing what will happen to me there. I only know that in every city the Holy Spirit warns me that prison and hardships are facing me. However, I consider my life worth nothing to me, if only I may finish the race and complete the task the Lord Jesus has given me – the task of testifying to the Gospel of God's grace.' (20:22–24) The last verse of Acts continues in a similar vein: 'Boldly and without hindrance Paul preached the Kingdom of God and taught about the Lord Jesus Christ.' (28:31)

4 It is the **Spirit's itinerary**. The Spirit gives specific guidance within the general command to take the word everywhere. It seems that a special vision was needed to open Paul's eyes to the fact that Macedonia should receive the Gospel. He was 'kept by the Holy Spirit from preaching the word in the province of Asia'. And when they came to the border of Mysia, they tried to enter Bithynia, but 'the Spirit of Jesus would not allow them to.' (16:6–7)

The controlling influence of the Holy Spirit in the mission of the early Church is plain to see. The book of Acts has rightly been described as the Acts of the Holy Spirit. The Church of today should be equally attentive to His promptings.

A CHURCH WITH STRATEGY

The sovereignty of the Spirit takes pre-eminence, but the Church's spiritual strategy is essential. The apostles had to use their minds to plan so that the Gospel would be established in the cities of the then-known world. There are at least three points to note:

1 The Jerusalem apostles **exercised strategic leadership**. Remarkably, after Stephen's death and the subsequent persecution of believers, the apostles themselves were still able to remain in Jerusalem. As churches became established in Samaritan and Gentile cities, the apostles took responsibility for their oversight.

It was one thing to know the mind of the Spirit, quite another to dedicate their lives to the service of God in preaching the

Gospel in city after city. Peter and John were sent to Samaria to confirm the work of Philip the evangelist (8:14–15). Peter was on mission in different towns and cities and was used profoundly in bringing the Gospel to the Gentiles (Acts 10, 11). Barnabas had a key role in harnessing the exceptional growth of the church at Antioch (11:22–26). And the Jerusalem Council acted wisely in overcoming the cultural barriers in the burgeoning Gentile church (Acts 15).

2   Paul's strategy was to **go to large centres** of population. From his base at Antioch he travelled many miles, evangelizing and establishing churches in Pisidian, Antioch, Iconium, Lystra and Derbe (modern-day Turkey). Paul's pattern was to go first to the synagogue. Those Jews and God-fearing people who accepted the message became the nucleus of the local church. He would then turn to the Gentiles. Eventually churches were founded in modern-day Greece and what used to be called Yugoslavia. With Asia conquered, he could make his way to Rome.

   Paul remained at strategic centres for long periods of time. He spent eighteen months at Corinth teaching the word of God (18:11). On reaching Ephesus, according to his usual pattern, he spent three months in the synagogue, but was hindered by their obstinacy. He then moved to the hall of Tyrannus with the converts. 'This went on for two years, so that all the Jews and Greeks who lived in the province of Asia heard the word of the Lord.' (19:10)

3   The object was to **strengthen** as well as **establish** churches. The apostles recognized the need to return to planted congregations in order to strengthen them. This is an important dimension that needs recovering in our day. The gifts of Christ (Ephesians 4:11–13) are crucial to a church planting vision – and also to a church maturing vision. 'They preached the good news in that city and won a large number of disciples. Then they returned to Lystra, Iconium and Antioch, strengthening the disciples and encouraging them to remain true to the faith.' (Acts 14:21–22)

   Leadership was key to a strong church, so suitable people

were selected by the apostles in order to oversee the believers. 'Paul and Barnabas appointed elders for them in each church and, with prayer and fasting, committed them to the Lord, in whom they had put their trust.' (14:23) This is also seen in the church at Ephesus (20:13–38).

WHERE AND WHY?

In Chapter 1 a number of reasons why a church begins to think about planting were explored. Case studies can be helpful when considering these points. Illustrations from the mainline denominations rather than the new churches stream follow, as it is the historic churches that need to reach their potential.

A KEY COUPLE WITH A VISION

When I was in Nottingham the first church we planted was in Lady Bay, a community of West Bridgford. It was an area with clear boundaries, always advisable when deciding where to plant. David and Mary Matthews lived in Lady Bay and I prayed regularly with them, as they were leaders of the youth programme. The idea of church planting had been discussed on a couple of occasions with them, but never very seriously. It had also been on the leaders' agenda for a couple of years, but no clear guidance had been forthcoming.

On one occasion, whilst in prayer at the Matthews' home, we were stirred by a scripture in the Psalms: 'The cedars of Lebanon will receive plenty of rain' (104:16). The scripture gripped us and had the effect of galvanizing the vision of a plant in that part of West Bridgford. Theologically I see no connection between this scripture and church planting, and would be very suspicious if someone else used it as their basis of guidance! However, we believed it was a promise that this community would receive the rain of the Holy Spirit if we acted upon the word, and I believe this has subsequently proved to be the case.

The verse, when shared, encouraged others and soon twenty-four people were willing to be part of the work. In the early days they called themselves The Cedars. I know that there was a great deal more motivating the situation than a few words from the Psalms, but it triggered the faith to get moving. For twelve months the congregation met mid-week in order to grow together and begin to make contacts in the community. At this point it was felt that the work required a full-time leader, especially as we were considering an independent church.

There were two men in the congregation who were willing to lead it. A member suggested that a day of prayer and fasting should be arranged to ask the Lord 'who was His choice?' The people that met together to share God's leading are an excellent example of how a church meeting should function. Most of those present explained that their human choice would be for Gordon Lingard, but God had clearly indicated David Matthews. Gordon was disappointed at not being selected, but soon recognized it was not God's time for him. He applied for a two-year theological course at St John's College, after which he was called into the ministry team at West Bridgford. David gave up his teaching job and became the full-time leader.

The group met initially in the Scout headquarters, then on a Sunday afternoon in a Methodist church, and are presently in a junior school on the main road of the community. They have always been a congregation of mostly young adults and have an emphasis on the 'poor and needy'. God spoke to them from Isaiah 41:17–20. This point should not be missed, because I'm sure this emphasis would not have emerged if the folk had remained in the central church. As we plant new churches, new expressions of 'being the Church' come to the fore as new leaders are given space to express their gifts.

DOWN AT THE DOG DAISY PUB

David Newton pastored the Conisbrough Baptist Church but wondered if God wanted to establish a new church in Mexborough, about three and a half miles away. He had written an article in the *Church Growth Digest*[1] about why working-class churches didn't grow very large, and as the Conisbrough church was 100-strong, he believed it was time to look for somewhere to plant. Unsuccessful attempts had been made at trying to 'bus' people out of Mexborough. It was clear that folk did not wish to travel to another church out of the town. David's desire was not to import Christians but, if possible, to create a church for the unchurched.

Conisbrough is a member of the Yorkshire Baptist Association and the need for a church in Mexborough was brought to their attention. Mexborough is the second poorest town in England, with 3,000 homes and 8,000 people. It was agreed that research should take place first. On a wet Saturday in March, a hundred volunteers from the Association visited all the houses and asked five questions. Of the 3,000 households, 1,400 were in. Of these, 600 said that a church was needed and 300 said they would attend. They estimated that about one in ten of the 300 would come to a service and that by the second week this might be halved. So, if their estimation was correct, there would be thirty on the first Sunday and fifteen on the second.

They wrote to the 300 homes and informed them that, in the light of the research, a new church would be starting on Easter Sunday. As a result of the questionnaire, the proprietor of the Dog Daisy Pub had invited them to use it for the worship service. This was an opportunity not to be missed. Fifty people attended the inaugural service and, interestingly, on the second Sunday it had reduced to twenty-five. In the last few years the church has moved to a portable building and will be opening a new church building soon. This will provide further opportunities for growth, as their present portable building is limited for space.

COME OVER AND HELP US

A few years ago a group of Cadets from the Salvation Army College in London carried out a survey in four roads in the village of South Woodham Ferrers, in Essex. They asked if a new Salvation Army Corps would be welcomed and if members of the household would attend. The answers were generally positive. George and Olive Anstead were retired and felt called to be actively involved in setting up a new church in the village.

The vision for this new work came originally when they were still active in the Wickford Corps. Olive had received a word from scripture which she believed was from the Lord. It was the verse from Acts 16:9, 'Come over and help us'. Paul knew he was called to Macedonia, and the Ansteads believed God was asking them to commit themselves to South Woodham Ferrers.

The next summer, Olive Anstead and a friend returned to the homes which had expressed an interest in attending a new church, inviting the people to a series of four 'cottage' meetings to be held in August. (A cottage meeting is a Salvation Army term for a house meeting which is open to non-members.) At the first meeting there were twelve people present, and over the next weeks the numbers grew. Encouraged by this response, they decided to begin meeting on a Sunday.

A church building, which had been unused on a Sunday, was hired and the first service was planned for October. The group believed that it was very important to make use of the media, so they notified local papers and radio, as well as displaying posters at key points in the village. They later discovered that this had attracted the attention of villagers and had even brought some to the meetings. Twenty-four attended the first service, which the Ansteads had decided would be informal. There was no band or choir, and there was freedom for sharing from the pew as well as the platform.

What has happened since? Three years later the Salvation Army purchased premises – a disused building belonging to the Church of England which was in need of refurbishment. A young people's group, numbering about forty-five, now meets on a Sunday at noon. During the week a junior choir and Tinbrel group are meeting – these children help to lead a monthly outreach. At 10 each Sunday morning a good number meet for prayer, which is followed by the service at 10.30, attended by more than forty adults (with a small band).

LED BY A DREAM

A decision was taken at West Bridgford that everyone should belong to a congregation. Those who met in the church building would still probably be the largest group, but we wanted to reflect truly one church made up of several congregations. This led ultimately to a weak centre, and later considerable time had to be given to strengthening the heart of the church. We learned an important lesson – that the centre, with all its resources, should be kept strong.

We had reached a place of confusion because, rather than looking for the strategic places to plant, we were merely dividing up the map of West Bridgford and asking our members to reach the people in their segments. Inevitably there were grumbles from members because they were unconvinced by this approach. Although we were committed to geographical evangelism, we had not taken into account that the congregation needed to know where the boundaries ended, and to have a sense of being a community.

Into this confusion one of the members shared a dream. Kevin Beevers had never shared anything like it before, and had been very reticent to do so. He had dreamed of church plants in two estates on the edge of West Bridgford – Abbey Park and Wilford Hill. Abbey Park had been established for about ten years, and Wilford Hill was under construction. When the leadership heard the content of the dream it was clear that this was strategic information, and we wondered how we had missed it. The older estate had no church building but had an Anglican daughter church on its periphery. There were no plans or land set aside for any church building on the newer estate. It was agreed that we should move towards planting a congregation on each estate.

There was no other word from scripture, but simply the peace of God that this was the right direction – particularly since this was where a huge number of people were living with no obvious Christian presence. The first congregation started six years ago and the second a year later. Neither of them have their own building; both use local junior schools.

WAITING FOR THE TIME TO PLANT

When Ray Whittle moved to Westborough United Reformed Church, Guildford, he was committed to the principle of church planting. Soon the church were committed as well, and they arranged for one of their members to be trained in the principle.

LEADERSHIP AND GROWTH

The Abbey Park congregation suffered from tensions within the overall church leadership when it was being planted. When there is a lack of spiritual harmony amongst the leadership it spoils the spiritual flow and blessing within the church as a whole. Abbey did not have the advantage of a full-time member of staff, as other congregations did, to provide a healthy foundation. To have the resources of a person with time and vision in the early stages is crucial.

The congregation has been a loving fellowship from the beginning, with encouraging worship, fellowship mid-week, and growth in Christ. In the first few years there was little growth through new people joining the congregation. However, they are now encouraged because, rather than losing spiritual direction and becoming complacent, there is life and growth among them. It is stronger today than it has ever been, and is still led by a lay leadership team.

The local junior school, used for Sunday worship, has become a very comfortable spiritual home. It is an attractive building, well maintained and in pleasant grounds. In recent years Abbey have planned annual weekends away. These have proved to be times when unity and vision have been deepened, refocusing them on the purpose for their existence.

PRAYER AND EVANGELISM

Abbey would admit that the corporate prayer life has not been strong over the years, but presently almost all the women, and a significant number of the men, are committed to prayer triplets.

The congregation is rediscovering the importance of evangelism at the heart of their corporate life. Many of the members recognize that it is only through the developing of relationships with neighbours that growth will come. In eighteen months there were eleven baptisms and now a number of younger Christians make up the congregation.

The children's programme has always been effective. Most of the congregation were asked to help in the Sunday School for short periods of time, whilst a smaller core of people were full-time. This has resulted in a lively faith in the children and 'held them' in the years when they are tempted to fall away. It now includes fourteen committed teenagers who serve in the congregation and attend centrally-organized, mid-week fellowship groups for young people.

Over the next three years questions were asked about where to plant and when.

A housegroup was started in Wood Street Village, about two miles from the main church. The group was asked to pray for their community and to be open to the possibility of forming the nucleus of a church plant in the village. During this time they studied a church–planting manual, *Creating Communities for the Kingdom*. [2] Ray was convinced of the principle and hoped that during this time the housegroup would begin to own the vision as well. This began to happen. In the summer a mission was held in the village and each of the 600 homes was visited. A number of questions were asked including, 'Would you value another church in the village?' Answers were generally positive.

It was agreed to plant in the village for several reasons. Firstly, they believed that every community needs evangelizing. Secondly, although there is an Anglican church in the village, it was served by a part-time curate. And, thirdly, they had received peaceful encouragement from the Holy Spirit to begin another church there.

The members of the mother church were asked to be involved in one of three ways:

- to commit themselves to belonging to the core congregation;
- to be a prayer partner of a core group member;
- to take an active and supportive interest in the new work.

The warden of an old people's complex offered the use of their lounge for the Sunday service and another building, not far away, for the children's work. The Sunday service began in October and a children's programme was added the following spring. They are considering moving to another venue as a more suitable building is required for the children's programme. As there are only three public buildings in the village, this may prove difficult.

The Wood Street church is a good example of quite a small mother church being willing to plant. Thus far, a good foundation has been laid for the future. Key to their willingness and motivation was the vision of their minister, and the training of one of their members.

NO MORE ROOM IN THE BUILDING

Nettleham is a large dormitory village of about 4,000 inhabitants, four miles north-east of Lincoln. In the last ten years Nettleham Methodist has experienced steady growth. Recently they believed that the Holy Spirit was leading them to a three congregational concept.

Several years ago the 10.30 a.m. service was consistently full, at times to capacity. It was clear that a decision needed to be taken so that growth would not be hampered because of limited space. The church experimented with a monthly 9.15 a.m. service to achieve two aims — to take pressure off the 10.30 service, and to minister to the needs of others who preferred a different type of worship service. This service soon became a weekly one. However, the 10.30 service became full again. What are they to do?

- Ask people to join the earlier service?
- Extend the building?
- Add a balcony?
- Relocate to a new building?
- Develop an evening service?

None of these were thought feasible. In their prayerful discussions the issue changed from providing more space to offering the ministries of the church to Nettleham Village. The vision of a third congregation, meeting possibly in a non-church building with a non-church cultured service, was born. It is being called a three congregation concept because the three services are all under the authority of the one church. They are endeavouring to express their unity in diversity.

Paul Shelton, the minister, discovered that the preferred meeting time for non-Christians in Nettleham was 11.00 a.m. on a Sunday. The new congregation began meeting in January with about thirty adults and thirty children. The services follow a monthly pattern:

- Week One, called the Interval, is a Gospel presentation using appropriate secular and Christian songs, drama and readings. This is coupled with a message that is designed to provoke questions rather than answer them. The basic concept is to encourage people to 'take time out' (hence the name Interval), and take stock of their lives.

- Weeks Two and Four are follow-up meetings, where the message given is orientated to non-Christians, expanding the Week One theme. These follow a more 'normal' church service pattern, but with explanation throughout.

- Week Three is left flexible. It can follow the same pattern as Weeks Two and Four, but it has also been used socially, for example going out for a picnic to deepen relationships with the new people.

In the first five months they made contact with about fifty people, of which around twenty came regularly. These came through personal invitation, with a conscious decision not to inform the whole village in the early stages.

A RETREAT LEADING TO ADVANCE

When the elders of South Parade Baptist Church, Leeds, met for a retreat day, God challenged them in particular directions. One was in the area of mission, and the other was a feeling that they were becoming too complacent. The church was growing and the fact that they were almost full on a Sunday morning meant that the sense of complacency was becoming dangerous. Was the Lord leading them to set up another congregation with a specific mission objective?

The church was informed and prayer encouraged. In July four members of the ministry team, led by David Morris, visited different areas of Leeds. In each place they looked at the volume of housing and the number of churches and possible meeting places. They also prayed in each of the four areas visited. They had begun the day with no preconceived notions as to which one would be right, but when they met at the end of the day they were unanimous. God was leading them in the direction of Adel. Adel was chosen for three reasons:

- There was only one church situated in the north of Adel, but none in their target area.

- A number of church members travelled past this location in order to get to the church at Headingley, so they had a place of mission nearer their homes.
- A new school had been built, providing an obvious focus of community interest.

Later, the information was presented to the church meeting and, after further exploration, was agreed. But how were they to test it?

- A questionnaire was devised and two houses in every street in Adel were visited to find out the character and needs of the area.
- They checked if the Adel Primary School would be available.
- Contact was made with the two nearest churches, Anglican and Methodist, to learn of their mission in the area.
- Information was shared with the Moortown Baptist Church and the Area Superintendent.
- They visited the Planning Department to discover any future plans for development.

By October the elders were able to bring the matter to the church. They clearly stated that the new congregation could only start if it received overwhelming support from church members, as the decision would have implications for the church as a whole. This support was duly given and the congregation started in Adel in February. As well as the twenty-five adults from the mother church, a further dozen were provided from Moortown Baptist. However, it was not envisaged that it should be a joint church project, but that Moortown members should transfer membership.

THE ECUMENICAL DIMENSION –
NOT PLANTING IN ISOLATION

Due to the DAWN movement and coupled with information in magazines, books and conferences, local church planting has been placed in a wider context. There is a certain amount of freedom, particularly as DAWN emphasizes 'planting after one's own kind'. Two or more churches can, therefore, work the same patch co-operatively without any competition.

As well as a geographical approach, very close attention needs

Not all of these will be relevant in every case, but mos
guiding principles. They are not in order of importance.

1 Is the location already being evangelized?
● There may be other churches in the area, but what is the overall population?
● Does the existing church(es) have an evangelistic strategy for the community?
● Can your church realistically begin to evangelize?

2 Are the majority of your church members in favour of planting?
● Has it been discussed and agreed in a church meeting?
● Is there sufficient understanding of what it will mean to the church as a whole?
● Have other alternative ways of evangelism been adequately considered?

3 Has prayer formed the foundation of the decision?
● How seriously have leaders and people sought the mind of God?
● Has God spoken prophetically? How has this been tested?

4 What research has taken place?
● How much do you know about this location?
● Has a survey or questionnaire been carried out?
● What are the needs of the community?

5 Is there a viable number of people to begin?
● Ideally this is thirty adults, more if possible. Do you have them?
● How reliable are these people?
● How well have they been prepared?

6 Who is going to lead it?
● Have they received any training?
● Are they strongly committed to the mother church?
● Do the planting group have confidence in them?

7 Is now the right time?
● What is your main motivation for wanting to plant a church?
● Are there 'pressures' to plant from a person/group which is influencing your decision-making?
● Would waiting another six months/year provide a better foundation? Or have you already hesitated too long?

8 Is there vision from God?
● Where has the idea come from?
● Is the vision in the church leader or the leaders and people as well?
● Is the vision strong and developing? Is it gaining ground in the church?

to be given to the ethnic minorities and cultural sub-groups within the nation. Kensington Temple are leading the way in planting churches to reach particular cultures within London. As well as the thousands who attend the multiple services at their central church, by the summer of 1993 they had planted about sixty satellite churches. Of these a number are for particular nationalities, for example Sri Lankans in South Harrow, Spaniards in Hampstead, Portuguese in Bayswater, and Eritreans in NW10.

SHINE is an example of a district strategy in St Helens, where thirty new churches are planned by the year 2000. SHINE (St Helens' Inter-church Neighbourhood Evangelization) is supported by most of the denominations in the area. After gathering data, church leaders identified the particularly needy areas of St Helens and set goals to plant three new churches by 1994, sixteen by 1997, and are praying for thirty by 2000. Through the inspiration of SHINE a number of other towns and cities have begun to think about their own district strategies. In Reading, the nine churches connected to Ditchdiggers have identified 137 communities of between 1,000 and 2,000 people and are developing plans to jointly resource the planting of these new churches. Their own training school will support and equip potential church planters, as well as other programmes for pastors, teachers, youth workers and missionaries.

It has become clear that the strategy of church planting is now the responsibility of the Church of Jesus Christ, and not solely in the domain of an adventurous church, however successful. God is speaking to His Church and saying that the harvest will only be gathered in as we each play our part. The basis of this is not a common doctrine or uniformity of approach, but a healthy respect for each other's expression of the Church and a whole-hearted commitment to evangelism and planting.

six

TAKING ROOT – HOW IT WORKED IN GUILDFORD

WHERE TO PLANT?

The Millmead Centre was committed to planting new congregations, but where and when? It was only a few months after my arriving at Guildford that different locations were being suggested for a possible church plant. There were about five different possibilities.

We were beginning to feel strongly motivated about a community called Guildford Park. There was already a church building which which was not used on Sunday, the Trustees being the Fellowship of Independent Churches. Before this idea could get very far we discovered that another Baptist church in Guildford had been asked by the Trustees to establish a work in the redundant building. I immediately contacted the pastor and told him of our plans. I assured him that as they were taking on the responsibility of Guildford Park we would support them in prayer. So, if not Guildford Park, where?

The elders gave themselves to extra prayer to decide where the first church plant should be. We informed the church of what we were doing and also asked them to pray. It was really between Onslow Village and Merrow Park Estate. Interestingly, Merrow has not featured very strongly since. There is value in being specific with the Lord and having His confirmation before you begin.

ONSLOW VILLAGE

About one and a half miles from the town centre one enters Onslow Village. It has about 4,000 residents, two schools and one church. All Saints Anglican Church has been at the heart of the village since the village was planned in the early decades of this century. No other denomination was represented. As we were sharing this information with those who might be involved from Millmead, I contacted the church warden of All Saints to inform him of our plans. I told him that no definite decision had yet been taken, but explained clearly the mission we had in mind. I spoke with the warden because All Saints were awaiting their new incumbent later in the year. I appreciated his warmth and good wishes, and he recommended that we use Queen Eleanor's School where he was the Chairman of the Governors.

BUT WHY ONSLOW VILLAGE?

- It is a clearly definable community.
- It has no Free Church representation and Millmead's emphasis would be different from All Saints.
- We sensed God's leading to begin. This came through God's peace within us and the confirmation of those wishing to be involved.
- It was where I lived. As I would be the one to 'get the congregation off the ground', being on the doorstep was a great advantage. I also needed to be willing to lead by example. If the church was to add a church planting ministry to its other Christian work, I wanted to demonstrate my commitment.

I have described how the group were chosen and how they gelled together more closely in Chapter 3. In this chapter I will outline what took place over a nine-month period, from October until June.

THE FIRST SERVICE

As early October approached the apprehension increased. Would any new people turn up? Twenty-four adults and fifteen children made up the initial core (five of those in the crèche). I had explained that we were beginning a long-term work, but everyone hopes for encouragements early on.

We needed to make sure that all the details were covered. The room was well prepared and welcoming. From previous experience, I was aware that rented buildings could look untidy when they have to be set up from scratch each week. People leave coats, briefcases, guitar cases, umbrellas, etc. lying around at the front. We did not wish to make the same mistake in this congregation. We had decided where to position the music group and the chairs. The table to collect literature on arrival, the cups, coffee and biscuits were all organized, and folk were available to welcome at the school entrance. The overhead projector was in good order and the acetates available. We wanted to start on time and also finish at the time stated on the publicity, so folk would remain for refreshments. When the length of the service is kept to one hour and fifteen minutes, the congregation remains for the time of fellowship afterwards.

The first service was an enormous encouragement. Samuel Chandra was being dedicated, so extra family and friends were present on this occasion. But what about folk who might come again next week?

We had been extremely encouraged on the first area visitation about five months earlier. As we were knocking on doors a couple passed us. Without us saying a word to them they said, 'We are going out, but we have received your letter and we are interested.' Door knocking is often very unrewarding, so to have two people take the initiative was almost unheard of. So would Derek and Lily come to the service? We had maintained contact with them in the following months and they had said they would come, but you can never be sure. Actually, they were there a good ten minutes before the start. They have made the point many times since that they were surprised at the warm welcome and the interesting content of the service: 'It wasn't like going to church, it was enjoyable.' These two founder members have been loyal from the beginning, helping in practical ways.

Who else came on the first morning? I had been telephoned by Doris a few months before the congregation began. Doris had heard that a new church might be starting. She and Stan live a few hundred yards from the school. We had visited and given them information of when the church would start and it was a joy to see this couple worshipping with us also.

Kate, who lived locally, and is in membership with the Guildford Community Church, also attended. She wondered if a local church would suit her as she wanted to become more involved in the community. When a person attends from another church I always make it clear that they need to tell their leaders. If in due course they wish to transfer, it can be done with sensitivity to both churches. After a few months Kate decided to become part of the Onslow Village congregation.

A family of four came. They had been invited by one of the core group because he knew that the husband was particularly interested in creation and evolution, the subject for the morning. This family came again at Christmas, but have not been since. Another lady was there, who has come on a couple of occasions, but has now declared herself not interested.

A teenager, Luke, also appeared. He was the son of one of the core group ladies, but he had stopped attending Millmead. Luke has come along faithfully, and with Owen has been particularly helpful in clearing the equipment away after the service.

A nurse training in midwifery wished to make it her church whilst training, and another elderly lady, Enid, appreciated the church being on her doorstep.

With the extra family members for the dedication, sixty-one people were present on this first occasion. It both surprised and deeply encouraged the new group. However, I think everyone recognized that it is one thing to start well, but another to keep going.

MORE NEW FACES

What happened in terms of attendance over the months? Every few weeks another new person came and, much to the delight of the congregation, decided to stay. The congregation is welcoming and the content of the services is relevant.

Joan noticed that Derek and Lily were walking to church and asked one Sunday in November if she could join them. Joan has become a very regular attender and speaks warmly of the spiritual help that she finds in coming. Joan's husband, Len, is unwell. We have been able to visit and support, and at times release Joan to go out by providing a person to be with her husband. As they are unable to tend their garden, a team of young people have given time to this.

Wyn came to us in November. She did not worship anywhere on a Sunday morning and again found a local church, to which she could walk, a great help. We had been concerned at the outset that more folk over fifty were needed to provide a greater age range. With the friends that had joined us, God had answered our prayers.

A local lapsed Millmead member, Geoff, began to come in November. Geoff had suffered a stroke and could only travel with the help of an electric car. He has subsequently started to attend another church regularly with his son. This is a better arrangement for him, but we still see him from time to time.

At the beginning of the new year Richard and Alison visited us with a new baby, Grace. It was the fact of us being a local church and small enough to make them feel welcome that attracted them. In June, when Grace was dedicated, the congregation was greatly increased with members from the respective families, none of whom are usually present in church. Alison is receiving one-to-one nurture and Richard is thinking deeply about Christian commitment.

Another Wyn came at Christmas and has continued to attend. She was brought along because she was the next door neighbour of one of the core group. Sheila appeared with her two children, Hannah and Alex, in March. She had made a commitment to Christ a few months earlier and was trying to find a spiritual home. It has been so encouraging to find folk come and put their roots down amongst us. In May, Helen attended with her daughter, Charlotte.

Interestingly, a number of other people who were originally part of Millmead have committed themselves to the congregation. They are people who live in the area, but for various reasons did not feel drawn initially. These include two university students, two families, and a single lady named Janet. It has also been encouraging to find a steady stream of visitors who, being in the area on a Sunday, have felt able to join us.

For pastors who want to plant a church as well as maintain their other responsibilities, what are the issues? Time allocation, members' expectations, and personal tensions should all be considered.

THE ONSLOW VILLAGE CONGREGATION

1 It was agreed by the elders that I should take responsibility for the new congregation. As it was recognized by the wider leadership that it was appropriate for me to do this work, it relieved some of the burden.

2 People knew that I was leading the congregation and, also, that my time commitment would diminish. This gave the group confidence that they weren't being sent out on their own, but also that my input would be limited in the long-term.

3 What was the commitment in the first six months?
   - Preaching about half of the time on a Sunday.
   - Leading mid-week life and overseeing most aspects of the work.
   - Working with a small planning team who would emerge as the main leaders.
   - Involvement in every aspect, up front and otherwise.
   - After six months I preached, and was therefore present, at the congregation once a month, but was still committed to some of the mid-week activity.

4 I was very conscious that I needed to 'be one of them' and not merely helping from a distance. As I live in the village and the work was a high priority for me, this was not difficult.

   I lived with the inevitable tension of trying to carry this responsibility as well as the growing, rather than diminishing, calls on my time at Millmead Centre. The congregation understood that I could not continue to give the same amount of time and leadership, but I had strong feelings of wanting to be supportive and 'with them' which cannot be fulfilled.

FREQUENCY OF SUNDAY WORSHIP

Each new church develops in its own way. There will be definite stages reached where decisions need to be made. For example, should the congregation meet every Sunday morning? I had

THE MILLMEAD CENTRE

1 I arranged for the preaching at the morning services to be adequately covered at the Centre. Although the teaching given was more than acceptable, there remain personal tensions. Worship produces a bonding between pastor and people, and this isn't easily replaced by filling the pulpit.

   At Millmead we emphasize team ministry, and this helps when a senior member of the team is away for several weeks. But those of us who lead churches are aware that being physically present on a Sunday adds as much as preaching the sermon. People miss you and you feel torn, but how can you be in two places at the same time?

2 If the mother church is going to remain the place with a strong central ministry, a senior leader cannot be away for too long a period. In Nottingham, where all the members belonged to a congregation, second-tier leadership could be developed in each of them. Those on the ministerial team could then function as teachers, evangelists, prophets, etc. in all of the congregations. At Millmead it is right for us to maintain a strong town-centre focus and, therefore, strength of leadership is required there.

3 We wanted to signal to the membership that planting churches is very important and not a ministry at the edge of church life. The best way to give this message was through me tackling the work. If key leadership people are not actively involved, church planting can be relegated to the desire of the few and the work marginalized.

   The added bonus is in reminding a local church that the Kingdom is bigger than what is taking place among us. This is recognized by most Christians, but through church planting the bigger issues of the Kingdom are before our eyes more naturally.

learned from experience in Nottingham that in the Cell-Congregation-Celebration model (see Chapter 7) commitment to the evening celebration can easily wane. Many Christians choose to worship only once on a Sunday. If a church wishes to remain one in worship and Spirit, they must have opportunities to be together. When a larger church divides into two or more congregations members quickly identify with their congregation and not the church as a whole. Ways need to be found to foster this oneness (see Chapter 7).

I presented the Onslow congregation with four reasons why I believed it would be advisable not to meet on the final Sunday of each month:

1 *It would lighten the overall burden and responsibility of the work*

A regular weekly responsibility is a heavy load to carry. Many of the congregation were taking on new responsibilities from scratch, and having one week a month free would obviously provide a rest.

2 *It would enable the congregation to keep in touch with Sunday morning worship at Millmead*

When a congregation has been planted and meets weekly, there is often resentment when called back to Sunday morning worship with the mother church. They have become used to worshipping with a known group in a particular area, and don't always see the need to worship with the whole church. So, to provide this pattern from the beginning removes possible tensions.

3 *The final Sunday in the month often coincides with half-terms and holidays*

If the group that is planted is small in number, it is better to recognize that at holiday times there may be fewer people present and not try to sustain the work on those occasions.

4 *The final Sunday in the month can be used for travelling*

In recent years a different pattern has emerged for Christians in that they tend to use some weekends to visit family and friends. This pattern, therefore, provides one weekend a month for them to fulfil these commitments, if necessary.

The Onslow group immediately saw the wisdom of these suggestions, and things worked well in the early months. We continue to monitor whether this pattern of Sunday worship is the most helpful, and will change to a weekly format if necessary. However, there are two related issues to bear in mind.

How easily will the children settle back into another children's programme once a month at the mother church? This has not presented a problem for us so far but it may do so in time. The final Sunday is often a family service at the Centre, which means that the children have no Sunday groups separate from the adults. In due course, we may have to organize the Onslow children's programme separately at the Centre.

What about the newer members who have never belonged to the sending church? We have found that some have attended Millmead on the final Sunday, and others simply don't attend church on that week. Also, what about those who aren't aware that there is no service on the last Sunday of the month? In all our literature we list the dates when a service is being held. Most people attend worship through invitation and friendship, very few simply 'turn up out of the blue'.

HOLIDAY CLUB

In this country, the numbers of children attending church on a Sunday have declined because of the secularization of society and changing family habits over weekends. Therefore, we have to find other times to care for children and to educate them with the Christian message. A home environment for about ten to twelve children is ideal.

In our early planning we decided to hold a holiday club in the October half-term. The village hall was the ideal venue and the schools received literature a few weeks before. It was made clear in the publicity that a Christian club was envisaged. We were hoping that as a result of the four afternoon meetings a few children would attend a weekly club in a home. The meetings were well attended with about fifty children. Some helpers came from Millmead, which lessened the load on local people.

We were able to start a Tuesday evening club called 'Powerpack', which ran from November until the end of May. One member, with a couple of helpers, ran the club in her home from 4.30 to

5.30 p.m. Those who came were mainly from non-churchgoing families. It is hoped to run another holiday club later in the year and the Tuesday evening meetings will resume in the autumn.

DAY-TIME BIBLE STUDY

A number of elderly people had begun to attend on a Sunday morning and we had to consider how to keep in contact with them during the week. We asked one member if we could make use of her home. This was greeted with resounding agreement and now, on a fortnightly basis, the group is gradually working its way through Mark's gospel. Mark was chosen because it lends itself to basic teaching and can be used evangelistically. I have usually attended this Bible study, but have asked another member to prepare the material occasionally.

SETTING THE GOAL

What did we believe was going to be achieved in the first year of the plant? We asked the congregation in October to pray about what numerical goal they had in mind. A deacon and fellow-leader of the congregation and I jointly agreed our numerical goal. Goals have value because they keep us from being vague. So much of our church life is not goal-related and therefore lacks a sense of working towards a given end. All of us know that we cannot produce spiritual life in others, this is the Holy Spirit's responsibility. But to ask the Lord specifically for a number of people to come to a knowledge of Him sharpens up our Christian faith and commitment. We agreed that we were prepared to pray for ten commitments by July and twenty by December. This was shared at a congregational meeting in November and owned by the group as a whole.

What do we mean by twenty commitments? It is often hard to measure what is spiritually taking place in individuals. Were we talking about brand new 'converts' or folk who were restored to a new faith? We were praying that people who had no previous background in church attendance, or had slipped away into a 'Wilderness' experience, should commit their lives to Christ. We believed that this should express itself in regularly attending the local church and becoming 'one' with the existing believers.

Actually, this was a very ambitious target. In the early days of a new church, time needs to be given to becoming secure and gaining an identity. So to have a high numerical goal as well was asking a lot of the people and the Lord. At about the same time I met a fellow pastor who had set a similar goal of twenty commitments for his church. The difference was, however, that they had 250 members. We recognized, as a congregation, that God would do His part if we did ours. This meant contacting and welcoming people to church, and praying for individuals specifically. Whether or not a goal is reached it is enabling us to depend on the Lord.

WAS IT REALISTIC?

As soon as a goal has been set, a certain pressure is felt. We need to resist the temptation to try to do the Lord's work for Him. We must not pick fruit until it is ripe. According to research carried out by John Finney,[1] it takes four years on average for a person to come to faith.

So what happened in the months up to June? Six committed their lives to Christ in significant ways. Another person made an initial commitment at a mission, and has been nurtured within the congregation. Several others are attending happily and are beginning to find a spiritual home. What do I mean by 'commitment to Christ in significant ways'? The following phrases have been used by those who have joined the congregation:

'I am more at peace.'
'I am more satisfied.'
'I never expected that I would ever want to go to church regularly.'
'I didn't accept the message when I first came, but now I do.'
'I have started to understand the Bible and want to read it.'

These are the words of individuals who are regularly at church and clearly open and growing in their knowledge of God.

There will always be those who resist the idea of goal-setting. But scripture does urge us to have faith, pray and preach the Gospel in order for people to be saved. If Christians are exercising a living faith and are making specific requests of the Lord, they presumably have some goals in mind.

THE SHAPE OF THE WEEK

Before beginning on a Sunday we had met as one large group, but what was the best way to organize ourselves once Sunday services started? In most churches a housegroup structure exists. There is tremendous value in dividing the congregation into small groups, but was a different structure required?

The congregation were asked how they wished to spend their time mid-week. Most recognized the need for prayer so two prayer meetings were organized each week for an hour. This meant that part of the evening could be used in other ways. Two groups met, involving a total of thirteen people. A third prayer meeting is being considered for folk who find it difficult to attend in the evening. To develop a depth of prayer in a smaller group is recommended. Another group wanted to study the Bible, so a fortnightly Bible study was arranged on a Monday evening. It was agreed that this meeting should also have an element of prayer.

A group of eight men decided to meet together to disciple one another on a fortnightly basis. We suggested that, as well as personal up-building, they should also have a village focus. This group met less frequently than originally planned, and arranged men's nights where friends were invited. The congregation is also blessed with capable musicians and singers. The music group meet once a week to practice, but are free in the week leading up to the final Sunday. It was recently agreed that they would also include time for prayer and study. Finally, a Tuesday morning group for ladies meets fortnightly, which centres on Bible study and prayer.

As we are still one overall church with Millmead, we try to arrange the congregation's mid-week meetings to avoid clashing with church meetings centrally. The mid-week groups have the usual features of housegroups, but the focus has an outwards bias as well as a pastoral aspect (i.e. prayer and interest in the community). Also, it is accepted that the pattern will change to meet the requirements of a growing congregation with different people and different needs.

PRAYER

I have personally found the mid-week prayer very encouraging. Over the months I began to pray specifically for many individuals,

You may know that the Guildford Baptist Church recently began a new congregation in Onslow Village and we meet on Sunday mornings at 10.00 a.m. at Queen Eleanor's School. (On the last Sunday of each month, however, there will not be a service.)

We are interested in this community and intend to pray for a couple of roads each month at the service and at other times. During November we will be praying for the people who live in Raymond Crescent and Queen Eleanor's Road. These will be general prayers for God's help, healing and protection, and for His peace to be experienced.

However, if there are any specific matters that you would wish us to pray for we would, of course, be happy to do so and would not mention you by name in the service or cause you any embarrassment. You can contact us with any request on 572745 in the evenings.

Sincerely,

Peter Nodding
Pastor – Guildford Baptist Church

Fig. 1 *Letter sent to specific roads in Onslow Village from time to time*

most of whom I did not know when we set out on this venture. These are people living in the village whom we have come to know through visitation. We always have space at the prayer meetings to cover personal needs and events that are taking place in our lives. Interestingly, this usually happens after we have concentrated on the needs of the village.

On a few occasions a letter has been distributed as another means of making contact with the community and assuring them of our prayer. We spend a couple of minutes in the service praying for people living in the roads of the village. The Church has a responsibility to pray for the spiritual health of the community.

CHILDREN

Children remain in the main congregation during worship for about thirty minutes. In October we had six children aged three to eight and four teenagers. As one of the teenagers stayed in worship and one helped my wife and the children, it left a teenage group of two. I would have thought that this was completely unworkable, but they have continued to come and share with a leader during their time together.

Teenagers do not fit easily into a new plant. At this age they usually like to feel part of a larger group. My son, who is thirteen, attends his own age group at Millmead after helping my wife with the children's programme, so maybe he gets the best of both worlds. In Nottingham, we found that most of the teenagers gathered at one of the congregations or came to church in the evening.

By June there were extra children in the crèche, fourteen in the three to nine age group and the same four teenagers. This has obviously meant that more people have had to commit themselves to the children's programme.

DELEGATING LEADERSHIP

Close involvement with a church plant is important, but it is also essential to delegate responsibility. How is this done? I have met regularly with one person on a Wednesday, where time is given to catching up on personal needs, any congregational business and prayer. As he is an elected pastoral deacon, he is the natural person to be second in command. He shares responsibility with another member who does most of the teaching. Other participants head up the worship, lead the children's programme, and share responsibility for administrative and pastoral aspects.

Most of the congregation are involved in serving in one way or another, but these particular members are those carrying leadership. At the outset I worked with this group in an informal way and they were seen as helping me. As my Sunday involvement lessened it became necessary to raise their profile so congregational members knew who to approach. At one of the congregational meetings these names were shared and information provided about their roles. The congregation were asked if they were in agreement, in order that they could give the leaders their full support.

Team leadership is essential. These five, with the help of their partners, will eventually plan the life of the congregation, whereas much of this responsibility was originally in my hands. I still believe it is right to maintain a leadership function myself for one important reason – I don't see a sufficiently strong evangelistic gift in any one of the leaders, committed though they all are to mission. They still need to grow in the desire and the ability to 'make it happen', and I will have to continue to provide this sort of input until such time as another leader emerges either from within their number or from outside.

SEEKER-FRIENDLY WORSHIP

The congregation are fairly flexible on a Sunday and adapt to those who wish to join us. We are careful to explain different aspects of the worship that may be confusing to those unused to church. On one occasion we were dedicating the child of one of the young couples who had joined us. We were informed that they had invited forty people to come, most of whom did not attend church regularly. Those leading on that day were flexible enough to arrange the worship and teaching in a way that was meaningful to all the visitors. The extra nine children were also catered for very happily within the children's programme.

VISITING

During the first year a second visitation of homes took place. In addition to this, the households received several pieces of literature about the congregation, which were simply posted through the letter-box. Over the next few years the publicity and regular visitation will continue. We accept that it will take a long time before many show any real interest in attending. It has been very encouraging, however, that through the regular publicity most of the homes have realized that there is a new church meeting in the village. This is only the first rung of the ladder, but has laid an important foundation for the future.

QUESTIONS

Questions will undoubtedly arise in any new church plant. The following two relate to Guildford, but could be applied to other plants.

1 *Is the congregation going to be successful?*

It would be true to say that the members are encouraged by the people who have joined us. A strong sense of family is present and growing, and all the congregation regard it as their spiritual home. I have no reason to believe that the congregation will not succeed. There is always a desire for many more people of course, and this leads to a sense of disappointment. However, the long-term nature of the work is recognized and, to a large extent, the growth is in our hands. Our commitment to prayer, witnessing, and really caring for people will be crucial to this growth.

2 *Did we start large enough?*

Although this doesn't seem to be an issue with the congregation members, I have wondered if we began with too few. Others have joined, of course, but asking some other folk to commit themselves would be a boost. I believe that we are weak at the level of natural evangelists, and presently, if several members are away on a Sunday, it is noticeable.

WHAT OF THE FUTURE?

Nine months on the congregation is prepared and committed to serve in Onslow Village. On average fifty-plus people gather on a Sunday and we believe that God will continue to add to our number. Of these, twenty-five were not part of the original group. We hold no illusions that growth will happen without real commitment. We are preparing another group to begin a congregation in Boxgrove, an estate in north-east Guildford. Thirty-four adults committed themselves to the original project and four more have asked to join from two other churches. Another couple from the Boxgrove area have committed their lives to Christ and wish to be part of this new congregation. The future looks good.

seven

MOTHER AND DAUGHTER TENSIONS

Some churches are planted with good preparation and according to the vision of the church. Others appear by default. Such churches come into existence through disagreement within a church over doctrine, worship, leadership or other issues. The grace of God remains constant and His desire to reach the world through His people covers many of our shortcomings as we offer Him our failure and repentance. Many splinter groups have gone on to thrive, but sadly others have folded because they have been badly birthed.

In our own church in Guildford we suffered a split back in the early 1980s, when a large number from the church left to form the Guildford Community Church. Since that time both churches have grown in different ways. It is most encouraging that we now enjoy a harmonious relationship at leadership level. This involves planning together and helping to run a full-time School of Evangelism with other churches.

We might expect tensions between mother and daughter when there have been disagreements and hurt, but the reality is that tensions can also exist when churches are brought to birth reasonably well. Two main points can help to reduce tensions:

- to be in agreement concerning the type of model to employ;
- a willingness to change the way the church is organized to further spiritual life rather than stifle it.

WHAT SORT OF MODEL?

At the planning stage it needs to be clear what sort of model is envisaged. Hoping that it will evolve on the way leaves the door open to potential chaos. Churches have run into difficulties when the group who are doing the planting lack clarity in the initial planning. There are no perfect models of how mother and daughters are to relate, but with commitment we can make most work. There are three types of relationship:

1 TOTAL INDEPENDENCE

From the inception of the plant the congregation know that in due course it will have its own leadership and handle its own affairs. This was the common way of planting amongst Baptists and others up until recently.

2 INTERDEPENDENCE

The new churches have recognized the value of giving the plant the freedom to develop and to take responsibility, but at the same time maintaining an important supportive link. This is the model that most new churches operate and gives freedom for apostolic and prophetic oversight.

Gerald Coates, Director of Pioneer People, employs this model and believes that his apostolic team should give direction in three areas:

- the appointment of leaders;
- decision-making concerning where to plant churches;
- overseas relief/mission.

The apostolic team are responsible for the doctrinal, moral and relational aspects of church life. This is all done through good relationships with the local church. The major responsibility for their local churches is in the hands of local leadership.

This model has obvious strengths. The new church is encouraged to stand on its own feet and take initiative whilst recognizing the wisdom and spiritual input that comes through gifted leadership from outside.

3 REMAINING ONE CHURCH WITH SEVERAL CONGREGATIONS

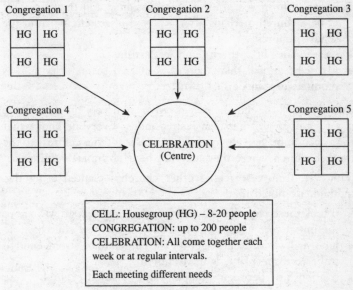

Fig. 1   *Cell-Congregation-Celebration*

Ichthus Christian Fellowship have made this model popular. However, they have found in recent years, with their growing number of congregations, that further sub-divisions have had to be made. They still have one central leadership, but it may have to be rethought as expansion continues. This model has been embraced by several other groups in the mainline denominations. The Cell-Congregation-Celebration model has been with us now for several years and is expressed diagrammatically above.

FINDING THE MOST SUITABLE MODEL FOR YOU

1 THE INDEPENDENT MODEL – ADVANTAGES AND DIFFICULTIES

What are the advantages and disadvantages of an independent model? Bob Smart, Ditchdiggers' leader, writes the following about independent churches:

'At first sight the concept of setting up independent churches seems appealing:

- easier to form – a group is commissioned and then set apart to be a church, perhaps after a period of resourcing from the sending church;
- clearer lines of authority and leadership;
- it can be argued that it brings a church to maturity as it is required to stand on its own feet.'

Added to this the members involved 'own' it very quickly. There is a high degree of personal responsibility. Everyone knows that they need to be actively involved, which is often a contrast to the mother church where they may not be. Bob Smart continues:

'However, from researching other churches planted using this method, we noted that:

- it took these churches some time to see any real growth above the initial core group sent to establish the new church;
- it normally took even longer for the church to be strong enough to be ready to plant its next church;
- relationship between mother and planted church were sometimes distant, rather than supportive (and therefore all practical help, finance, giftedness and other resources dried up);
- in some instances the motivation for planting the church was questionable (i.e. a group separating because of doctrinal differences, a disagreement over leadership, direction, etc.).'

There is no right model and each fellowship will have to find the one that most suits them. To plant strong independent churches is an effective way to evangelize. An example of a well-planted, independent church with few tensions with the mother is Bretton Baptist near Peterborough.

Beginnings

The ministerial team of Harris Street Baptist Church, Peterborough began to survey the Bretton area of their district to discover if it would be a suitable place to plant. Several of their members already lived in Bretton and the church made it a matter of prayer. The small township had only been built six years earlier and so everything was new — fertile ground.

The first confirmation, in practical terms, to plant in Bretton came when the junior school was opened. The church was given permission to use the hall for worship and so in the early 1980s fifteen people gathered for their first service in the new plant. From that small beginning the work grew rapidly. In just six months they had outgrown the school hall and were able to move into the new community centre that had just been completed. By this time fifty to sixty people were attending every Sunday morning. The community centre provided several rooms and so a good teaching ministry to the children was provided.

Independence

Bretton maintained close links with the mother church, appreciating their guidance and support. They shared baptismal facilities until they hit upon the idea of using the school swimming pool nearby. They remained in membership together for two years, until the move to break away from the mother church followed confirmation from the Lord. There were few tensions in the process and the one church became two.

Bretton Baptist Church became independent with thirty-six names on the Covenant of Founding Members. As such they had to take responsibility for their own finances, including an outstanding loan of £6,000 on the manse and payment of their minister's stipend. The work was recognized by the Baptist Union Home Mission Fund which provided them with an Initial Pastorate Grant and decreasing loans over the following ten years. Within a few months of going alone the church began to hold an evening service as well.

Resources

In order to serve the Lord more effectively in Bretton, they began to explore the possibility of having their own church building. Next door to the community centre was a piece of barren land on which the local authority had intended to build a school. Some two years previously a group of ladies had been praying in a house opposite and had asked the Lord to give them the land for a church building. Bretton's treasurer was appointed as building overseer and was given full responsibility for negotiating with Peterborough Development Corporation, assisted by other members of the diaconate.

New building

Although their first request for the land was turned down, it was finally offered to them – three-quarters of an acre at £8,600. The offer, at one-quarter of the land value, was on condition that they complete the building within three and a half years. After much discussion, but mainly prayer, they decided to go ahead, and six months later had paid for the land in full.

Now to put the building up! The architect was appointed and plans drawn up. It would cost them £280,000 to build. The small, believing fellowship continued to look to God to provide. The local paper by this time was getting interested but couldn't understand why the church held no fund-raising events. However, they wrote an article under the headline 'God will build our church' which gave the church a great deal of publicity. Six firms were invited to tender and six months later they had a revised target of £275,000. On paper, with the loans and funds promised, they were just £4,000 short of the full amount. Of these funds £80,000 was from promised gifts within the fellowship. Every individual had been challenged to step out in faith to promise to give towards the building over the next four years. Not only had they grown in numbers but in faith!

Every aspect of the financial position was dealt with thoroughly, including the required cash flow. The bank manager discussed with them a £120,000 bridging loan with the possibility of this being at cost.

Up it goes

Building began in July. The people worshipping in the nearby community centre were able to watch every brick being laid. Although caught up in church affairs, the emphasis on outreach continued and by October they were literally bursting at the seams each Sunday. Church membership had risen to seventy-six.

The church was finally completed and they moved into their new building in time for Easter Sunday the following year. Ten people were baptized that day, but the joy of the fellowship was tinged with sadness as their leader was taking his last service. Having planted and been part of establishing an independent church in Bretton, he felt it right to move on.

The new minister joined them in January and their membership continued to grow. By December the following year they had reached a hundred. At the same time they were able to come off the Home Mission Fund Pastoral Grant, after only five years out of the ten allowed. Their finances have continued to be healthy. The church did not need to take any part of the bridging finance it negotiated, but some loans remain to be paid off.

Up to date

Bretton Baptist Church is continuing to grow under their minister. Membership is now 120 and since the early 1990s they have had to hold two morning services because of pressure on space. Now, in turn, they are themselves considering the whole matter of church planting.

2 THE MULTI-CONGREGATION MODEL – ADVANTAGES AND DIFFICULTIES

When we first considered planting a church in Nottingham the only model in our minds was independence. The folk involved were ready to accept that this was the way forward for them. It was only after my sabbatical research that other possibilities came into focus. I shared my findings with the whole church. This included the first congregation, who had not become independent at that stage. There was immediate agreement that we should adopt the one-church-with-several-congregations model. It was a personal joy to learn that those who had set out on the course of independence were delighted to accept this new idea. They believed that they could function as they had been, but with all the added benefits of the resources of the mother church.

Since then the advantages and difficulties of this model have been analysed. David Goodyear, in *Church Growth Digest*, describes his own church in Taunton in an article, 'One Plus One = One'.[1] In addition, a Baptist Union survey compiled by Roger Sutton and Adrian Argile[2] discovered the following advantages:

- It keeps the people together as one unified church. When it works well, there is the feeling of being united and yet also diversified.

- It creates the missing church element in the Cell-Congregation-Celebration model. This is particularly relevant to churches with a membership of over 200, where the congregational element is missing. The congregations meet in the morning in their areas and in the evening come together, if there is a large enough building, for a celebration for all. It incorporates the bonuses of a large fellowship and also the value of meeting in a congregation, where one can know most people.

- It is a good use of resources and personnel. The full-time team operate over all the congregations and can give specialist input at central times of teaching and as required in the congregations.

- The same pattern of success achieved at the mother church is easily repeated in its congregations.

- By far its greatest success is the model's ability to localize evangelistic concern – particularly helpful for the church which draws people to it from a large catchment area. It makes such people more aware of their neighbourhood and encourages them to pray and be involved locally.[2]

This is the model that we employed at West Bridgford where we remained one church, but with several congregations. It is also the one we are working with in Guildford. We discovered the reality of the above points and were convinced of the usefulness of this sort of approach.

However, there are seven possible areas of difficulty:

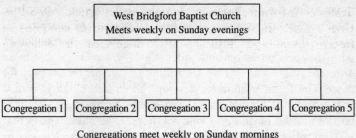

Fig. 2   *Multi-congregation model*[3]

When is a church not a church?

The congregation can feel itself to be simply an extension of the mother church, and not really a church at all. Consequently, taking real responsibility for the life of the church can be stifled. It can express itself in too great a dependence on the central leadership.

Certain decisions are made by the local congregation, such as evangelistic strategy and organization of the internal church life, but other decisions are in the hands of the elders or the church as a whole. This can lead to frustrations among the members of a congregation and the feeling that 'we are not allowed to do what we want'. This led to two of the Nottingham congregations becoming independent. One is the only church on a new housing estate and has called its own minister. They worship in the local school, but are considering purchasing land for their own building. The second only decided to become independent recently so their plans are not fully clear.

In both cases, the decision to become independent was not without tension. In addition, not all the members who made up the different congregations were agreed about the best way forward. Some wished to remain with mother and some didn't. As the matter could not be resolved individual members were asked to make a personal decision, which meant some returned to the West Bridgford Baptist Church.

If a congregation wants to become independent, this need not be considered a failure. Indeed, those adopting this model should be prepared from the outset to enable one or more of the plants to go out on their own. However, in the early days in Nottingham I did not see it this way and suffered a measure of heartache. If possible, the process of independence should take place harmoniously, with supportiveness on both sides. God's grace will cover these differences of opinion if we are willing to encourage and pray for those who leave, wishing to develop the church on their own.

Integral to this model is one vision which is working itself out on the ground in different congregations. The advantage is that each member knows that they are part of a church which is a great deal bigger than their own congregation. They are sharing in a far-reaching vision and have access to the training and resources. The congregation is acting as a church in almost every way except in having its own final autonomy and government. David Goodyear argues that this was probably the situation in the early Church.[4] Paul addressed his letters to the Church at Corinth, and Thessalonica, etc. There must have been many different places where the Church met in these cities, but they were addressed as one.

Although many members are totally convinced of the advantages of the one-church-several-congregations model, as a church grows a number of members will argue the case for independence. To review the situation openly from time to time will reveal what is happening in individual congregations and guide what is the best next step. Independence may arise because of one of the following:

- A different vision emerging in a congregation – this is not only about theological emphasis or vision, but the way the church is to be run.
- A loss of confidence in the overall church leadership – this may be a result of a breakdown in communication arising from insufficient freedom to develop a congregation's plans.
- The geographical distance between mother church and the congregation – people find it easier to pledge loyalty to their own community and not another one several miles away.

Maintaining relationships

Relationships between overall leadership and the congregations need to be kept in good heart and lubricated with prayer and fellowship. This means meeting together regularly, and leaders throughout the church (central and local) emphasizing corporate and not personal vision. There was tremendous unity and visionary times with the leadership of the congregations in Nottingham, where it was more fully developed. The sense of being together in an important work for the Lord is special.

Several times a year a wider group of leaders should meet to share vision, iron out communication weaknesses, and hear what is happening in the church overall. It is on these occasions that potential 'primary-tier' church leaders are encouraged to grow. Good relationships are at the heart of the Church, and this model will only work effectively in an atmosphere of love, trust and mutual accountability. As the quality of the relationships wane, so will the witness of the Church.

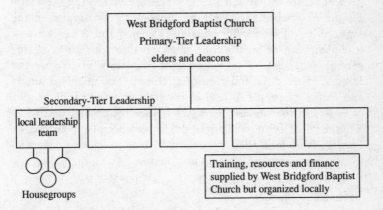

Fig. 3   *Multi-congregational leadership structure*

The quality of second-tier leadership

This model allows freedom for the biblical concept of delegation to flourish. As the church continues to plant, for every member ministry becomes a reality. There is more than enough for everyone to do. Finding the right leaders and equipping with training is essential. It sometimes requires considerable patience for the person in the pew to encourage those who are in the process of developing their ministries.

How are members going to develop unless we give them opportunities to serve the Lord in significant ways? We have developed a professional class of ministers in our churches, with most of the workforce redundant. God never intended it to be like this. Roger Forster of the Ichthus Christian Fellowship said that many years ago he had to make an important decision: 'Am I going to grow my own ministry, or the ministry of others?' Ichthus is a testimony to the fruitfulness of his conviction to grow the ministry of others. Although it can be a great deal easier to do things ourselves, it misses the New Testament vision of the Body of Christ and every-member ministry.

Training is crucial because the quality and gifting of the second tier of leadership taking place in the congregation may fall far short of those who lead centrally at celebrations. Those who were present before the church started planting congregations can long for the days when they were guaranteed a good sermon in the atmosphere of wonderful worship. Further, the congregational leadership can be significantly depleted through resourcing the central eldership. The dangers of weakness at second-tier leadership are clear and require attention. The quality, training and choice of people to lead in congregations is crucial.

Paul said to Timothy, 'don't lay hands on anyone hastily' (1 Timothy 5:22). Paul recognized the importance of appointing the most suitable leaders as it is relatively easy to appoint a person, but far from easy to 'dis-appoint' them.

So far and no further

This model works best when it operates within the boundaries of a clearly defined community or geographical region. When the distance between mother and plant becomes too far, problems of communication and an unwillingness to travel to central events can arise. Members have a sense of belonging in their own community and with what is happening spiritually in that area. Travelling out of their community does not have the same attraction when something of spiritual substance is planted in their area.

It may be that this model will have to take on a different shape once another set of congregations have been established in a neighbouring community five or ten miles away. It could still be working out one vision, but interdependently, with more than one leadership team.

Communication

When most of your members are sitting in church on a Sunday morning, communication is relatively easy – yet even in these situations people complain that they have not been informed. But what happens when the church is meeting in three or more places on a Sunday morning? There is an evening celebration, but not all will attend due to family commitments or no desire to worship twice on a Sunday. How do you communicate the wider vision, over and above what is happening in the local congregation?

We found it very helpful in Nottingham to appoint congregational workers who voluntarily gave up a couple of days a week to administration, pastoring and helping the congregational leader. These willing folk met once a week to pray and receive an update of important news. This was then communicated on the following Sunday morning. Such folk were vital links in the chain in keeping the communication channels open.

Key leadership

Ichthus has survived and continued to grow because of the strength of its central leadership team. God's way is for leadership ministry to reproduce itself over and over again. Key leaders must be committed to reproducing strong leaders.

There is no question that there is a heavy reliance upon the person(s) who has given the vision, and through their gifting and faith brought something into being. Church-growth philosophy discovered that longevity of ministry both maintains and deepens a local church's work. This is true as long as the church leaders are growing and developing themselves, otherwise they are a bottle-neck.

God anoints people, not buildings or movements, with His Holy Spirit. It is Spirit-filled leaders, who have learned to delegate and train, who will envision ongoing church planting.

Appointed by leadership and agreed by the congregation, the congregational worker is the link between the two and is responsible to the congregational leader or minister. The work involved is administrative/pastoral and needs to be done with an evangelistic outlook. It involves:

1 Meeting on a regular basis with the administrator to receive and give updated information such as:

    a) changes in addresses of members or other information;

    b) dates of congregation meetings or events which need to be put in the notice sheet or have a room booking;

    c) dates when not meeting at usual venue, i.e. school holidays, etc.;

    d) report names of new people attending congregation;

    e) names of those wishing to attend membership and baptismal classes and those who are brought into membership at the congregation.

2 Passing on information and instructions for housegroup leaders, Bible study material, etc.

3 Being available to meet regularly for prayer.

4 Being an enabler and delegator of tasks which need to be undertaken in the congregation. Especially to be the 'eyes', noting any new faces or those who have been irregular in attendance for various reasons.

5 Being a contact person for the congregation in a variety of ways, thus relieving the congregational leader of some of these responsibilities.

Keep strong at the centre

Be careful to avoid the danger of becoming too weak at the centre. If numbers or resources become limited at base, the rest of the work will suffer. It is possible to spread out too quickly, trying to fight battles on too many fronts. This is not to say that the centre is more important than the congregations – both are integral to the vision. However, they are performing two different functions. The centre has to be as evangelistic as the congregations, but at the same time maintain its reserves so that it can resource and encourage.

A church needs to choose its model and make it work. The above is not the only model, but it is the one with which I am most familiar. However, there is great value in the interdependent model, especially if leadership relationships can be maintained and respected.

WHAT ARE THE TENSIONS IN THE MOTHER?

When a number of congregations have been sent out from the mother, what sort of feelings does she have? It is often not appreciated when church planting first starts, because there is so much concentration on those being sent out. Some tensions are felt by leaders and others by the people.

1 LEADERS

- A difference of theological emphasis may arise between mother and plant. Indeed, possibly the main reason that a plant has been suggested is because of lack of theological agreement in the church. Either a spirit of unity should be found or the plant will have to become independent.

- If some members of a leadership group aren't really convinced or committed to church planting their relationship with the evangelistically minded group who have left to plant will be strained. The planting group require strong endorsement from leadership. If it is not forthcoming, misunderstanding and possibly separation will result.

- From the outset it needs to be clear who is leading the church as a whole. In the early days of any plant, mother church leadership should hold the spiritual reins. Very quickly after a new church has been planted its leadership exercise a lot of authority. If clear lines of leadership responsibility are agreed at the outset, a vying for spiritual authority in the two congregations can be avoided.

- Great care needs to be taken when selecting leaders for the plant because some individuals want to be a 'big fish in a small pond'. When this happens tension may not be easy to overcome. The people to recognize and appoint are those who have leadership gifts and are loyal and committed to the overall leadership, rather than those who are independently minded. Enthusiasm for a suggested church plant is important but must be free from a desire to use the plant to exercise a significant personal role and to have influence with people in a smaller group.

Unity between mother and daughter is fundamental. Respect and support for mother church leadership is implicit in a 'well-birthed' church. The person will not cause tension if he/she is in spiritual harmony with the sending church's leadership. Therefore, those to guard against include:

a) Those whose pastoral gifts draw people to depend upon them and not on the Lord. This is the beginning of a separatist group.

b) Those who have shown evidence of not having a teachable heart. All of us need to be in submission to the wisdom of brothers and sisters who lovingly point out our weaknesses.

c) Those who openly and persistently criticize church policy and the leaders in particular.

- Who is going to take responsibility for the jobs that now need filling because some of the best people have left? The positive side is that others rise to the challenge who may not have had the opportunity. However, losing a key person who is performing a central job, like youth teaching or administration, can be hard to accept.

2 THE PEOPLE

- It feels more exciting to go out than to be left behind. There are a number who will not want to go out because they are secure at the centre, and others who regret having to wait for their opportunity to begin a congregation in their locality.

- Friends will no longer sit together because they will be somewhere else. Although this may appear to be a small cost in the light of what is being achieved, those remaining feel the loss strongly.

- The church might have been comfortably full and now it isn't. This can be a discouragement for those remaining. However, it is also a challenge to fill the places again. When we first planted in Nottingham the empty seats were filled again very quickly. I wonder if the Lord is just waiting for us to be more adventurous so that He can bring in new people?

- When this has happend more than a couple of times the mother church can begin to feel like the remnant, even though they are still quite large. Those who remain know why people are being sent out, but psychologically it can feel worse.

Leaders should prepare the members for these feelings and encourage them to be as pioneering as those who have been sent out. Geraldine Clark, Administrator at West Bridgford observes, 'Fortunately I, and others who have been through this process before, know that God will raise up new leaders, new people will join us, and congregational life will go on with or without the group who have left us. Part of the challenge to the remnant is to remain faithful and strong. To be a praying, loving and welcoming congregation which will attract new people to their numbers.'

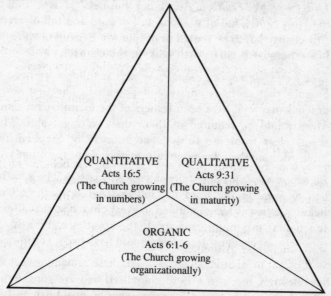

THE HEALTHY CHURCH: Growing equally in all three areas at the same time

Fig. 4   *Total growth in the Church*

ADAPTING THE ORGANIZATION

A church should be growing in three ways: qualitative, quantitative and organic growth are each important. Most of us understand the value of growing in numbers and in our Christian characters, but often overlook organizational growth.

Acts 6 is an excellent illustration of the early Church adapting in order that further growth can take place. Neglect was evident in two areas. The Greek widows were being overlooked in the daily distribution of food, and the apostles were too busy at the expense of the word of God. The result of these roles and structural/ organizational changes was numerical growth. Many priests became obedient to the faith (6:7), Stephen witnessed to his own culture (6:8), and Philip the Evangelist (one of the deacons) exercises an extremely powerful ministry in Samaria (Acts 8).

HOW DID THEY RESOLVE THE PROBLEM?

- *Look for people of fullness.* Acts 6 is a 'full-ness' passage. Full of the Holy Spirit, full of wisdom, full of faith and full of grace. Any change has to be rooted in people who are full of spiritual life, otherwise it isn't worth making the changes.

- *Look for people who are capable.* As well as fullness we need to be sure that there is ability and potential. The first seven deacons may well have been leaders of the Gentile Christians. More would be required of them than serving tables. This seems clear from the subsequent ministry of Stephen and Philip, despite there being no information about the other five.

- *Encourage people to concentrate on their primary job.* The apostles had to minister the word of God and not serve the tables. Regular review is recommended in every church so that all will function at maximum capacity. If the apostles had not made these crucial changes, Jerusalem would have had a bottle-neck situation.

What does this mean in a local church? If you are considering church planting it is going to mean organizational change. It is dangerous to have church structures that are too fixed, or a constitution that is too prescriptive. On a few occasions since coming to Guildford, God has spoken to us about being flexible and adaptable to the movements of His Spirit. A church needs to be taught to find their spiritual security in Christ and not in their role or a church's pattern of ministry. It is obvious where a person's security lies when the suggestion is made to rethink their meeting or their position.

Whenever changes are considered the church should be well prepared for them and explanation given as to why they are being suggested. In the last couple of years at Millmead we have made a number of organizational changes. What were the reasons for these?

1 *Decision to have two morning services*

Problem: Overcrowding. Visitors not able to sit in the church. It is accepted that if a church is full some folk don't bother to come again because of lack of space.

Result: Adequate room for visitors and potential new members. Needed to provide more children's workers, more musicians, more stewards, etc.

2 *Decision to plant congregations*

Problem: Much discussion for several months/years about the best way forward with no clear conclusion, i.e. bigger building or church planting.

Result: The body of the church committed to this form of evangelism. Beginning to help members to focus on local communities.

3 *Planting a congregation*

Problem: Deciding where we should plant. Helping those members who lived in the vicinity of the proposed first plant to come to a decision. Rethinking their housegroup emphasis.

Result: New congregation. Local people attending. Those involved have a commitment to evangelism locally.

4 *Changing the nature of the diaconate*

Problem: Under the previous structure the elders didn't share closely with the deacons because this was not required in the way the ministry was organized. New deacons were needed to oversee other spiritual functions in the church.

Result: Monthly prayer and sharing with elders. The new diaconate was recognized as a second tier of leadership to oversee their particular function on behalf of the elders and the church. This change also involved altering the area structure which had become largely administrative and pastoral. The emphasis changed to be more community focused.

The reasons for the changes can be summed up in the phrase: *outward and Kingdom* and not only *inward and Church*. Structural changes do not only change the direction of individuals, but should help the whole church to operate differently. In January we called the church to a month of prayer and fasting. This didn't mean no food for all for thirty-one days, but that every meal time was covered by several people fasting. We recognized that there is no lasting value in making organizational changes if God is not changing *us* to flow with the changes. It is a reminder of Acts 6 again: the structures of the church are to be serviced by the right people, full of the Holy Spirit, in order to provide time and gifts for the salvation of the community.

FERTILIZING FOR GROWTH

Ruddington Baptist Church in Nottingham had struggled for years until 1980. In that year the membership was thirty-nine, a number of whom were too ill or old to attend. Morning service worshippers numbered between twelve and fifteen, with about twenty-four attending in the evening. It was a traditional church but with only two couples with children. Even one of those was contemplating moving for the sake of the children. The church was resigned to its dying state. Those people who came to find a spiritual home would not return because they were looking for a fellowship which was more 'alive'. However, it was a friendly church and members always gave of themselves if they could meet a need.

Ruddington was like many churches in which disillusionment has set in and where there is little prospect of change. These churches maintain a regular worship service, there is a loyal core, but radical changes need to take place if they are to serve the community with a living Gospel. What role does a planting church play in this situation? Most of their membership is taken up in fulfilling their own vision, but it may be that there are the resources and people to help. Instead of planting a new church where one already exists, they can help to bring the existing church to life. There are instances where it is not possible to help the church that is already in the community, and another church may have to be planted alongside it. But every effort should be taken, in the first instance, to work in harmony.

We call this resuscitation. Re-potting is another helpful image. As well as having a vision for new churches, there is potential to revive old ones. A church that has been struggling in the doldrums for years can be resuscitated from within through a change of leadership or a new minister being called. However there are ways in which a church from the outside can help. Whilst in Nottingham we were able to help several local churches, not only to strengthen their witness but also to become strong churches in themselves. What are the important factors on both sides?

FACTORS FOR THE SENDING CHURCH

EARNING RESPECT THROUGH RELATIONSHIP

Small churches are sometimes suspicious of the so-called 'successful' church. They can feel that if they get involved with them they will be taken over by 'Big Brother'. So, relationship must be the only foundation from which help is shared. The attitude of the people who come from the helping church will either strengthen the relationship or stifle it. The attitude must not be, 'We know what you need! The only way that any spiritual life will develop in your church is through *our* input! You need our help. Take what we are offering on our terms. You need to come under our authority before we can help you.' If this is the message that a church hears they may accept the help, recognizing their own need, but the real foundations needed for a strong work will not be built.

Good lessons will already have been learned by the helping church and, because God has blessed them, they will be able to encourage spiritual life in the smaller church. But attitude is key to the relationship. To show loving interest in the members as people, discovering who they are and where the church is spiritually, is not only right but Christian. This relationship process may take several months, whilst trust grows. During this time preachers can be provided and mid-week help, as appropriate. In the case of Ruddington, West Bridgford Baptist provided several preachers and also a person to lead a mid-week Bible study. The lay pastoral assistant at West Bridgford showed a loving attitude and spirit of helpfulness and was greatly appreciated. More importantly, he prepared the way for a far deeper relationship in the future.

WILLING TO SACRIFICE

The primary sacrifices are people and money. It is one thing to provide a preacher who is going to return to his home church next week, but it is another to send a person to the church to become part of their fellowship. It is encouraging for a church to receive a love offering, but it is even more encouraging to receive regular financial support to sustain their ministry.

1 *Giving away your best*

In 1980 we called Peter Jackson to be a student minister in West Bridgford Baptist Church. He was training with Northern College on their alternative pattern of training, a course where a student looks after a church as well as undertaking two days of residential training each week. As we were to call another minister full-time in 1981, the college suggested that Peter be placed at another church so that he could exercise more responsibility.

The biggest sacrifice that I have ever made, in terms of losing a ministry gift, was to give Peter away to the church at Ruddington. It was agreed that he would exercise his ministry there for the half week that he was free from study. The sacrifice was two-fold: I enjoyed a good working relationship with him; and he was making a significant input into the life of West Bridgford, which would end. I wonder what the church at Antioch felt when the Holy Spirit said, 'Set apart for me Barnabas and Saul for missionary work' (Acts 13:2)? Clearly they were valued as prophets and teachers at Antioch, and the church would have liked to have kept them.

God has bigger purposes than most of us understand. The most productive growth for certain key leaders is for them to go to another church. It is only when certain people are no longer there to be relied upon that other members can grow into their shoes. Who filled Paul and Barnabas' shoes in Antioch? We need to be open to God's voice so that we know the ways in which He wishes to move His servants around.

In any living fellowship strong leaders will be emerging. An openness to God's Spirit is required so that we can see how to use these leaders most effectively. Some who have led a housegroup, headed up a particular department of the church, shared in the up-front teaching and leading, or proved themselves in other ways may be being equipped to take on more significant responsibility. As there is a limit to the number of key positions in most church structures, the Lord may be leading these potential leaders to serve in another church. Of course, they will be used if the church begins to plant other churches because extra leaders and gifts are needed in abundance. But even in these churches, leadership gifts are to be given away.

2 *Money as well*

When Peter Jackson became the student minister at Ruddington, he was supported entirely by West Bridgford Baptist. The fellowship should be commended because, although we did not receive much from Peter during his years of training, there was no sense of 'not getting our money's worth'. Financial help continued for six years until Ruddington became self-supporting. The reason that a church is willing to make these sort of financial sacrifices is simply because of the relationship with the person. If Ruddington Church had called a person unknown to us, we may not have been so willing to provide the money. It is the fact of knowing and loving a gifted member of the Body of Christ that enables faith to be released in support, and so God extends and builds His Kingdom.

The investment in Ruddington has been rewarded. The church is now strong in the village, has grown steadily, and presently has about 120 attending on a Sunday morning. They have established outreaches in the community. Honeycomb is a shop witnessing to God's love and justice in practical ways, and The Lantern Restaurant exercises a concern for the whole person, as well as being a base for evangelism.

All denominations are asked to fund their own home mission work, and of course this is right. However, a local church feels so much more part of the ministry in another church when one of their own is serving there and they are helping to foot the bill.

SHARING RESOURCES

Because a member of the sending church transfers to another church, resources can flow more easily. The leader becomes the catalyst, uniting the two fellowships. The one who is receiving the help knows that the sending church are not interested only in furthering their own work, because they have demonstrated their commitment. What sort of resources were West Bridgford able to provide to the different churches?

1 *Musical help*

It was decided that a gifted worship leader would help to lead a Sunday afternoon monthly 'Songs of Praise' at Kegworth. This helped to add to the church in the village and introduced a host of new worship material into what was a very traditional church. An organist transferred to Ruddington for a period of time to play on Sunday mornings.

2 *Missions*

A twenty-plus group from West Bridgford led a mission at Kegworth during the summer months. A three-day evangelistic mission was held at another church using those gifted from the sending church.

3 *Advice*

We are only as wise as the people who make up our local church. Help was provided concerning property and finance matters. Each person who took a leadership role in another church, as part of their ministry training, had a support group. These groups of about seven people were a mixture of members from West Bridgford and the other church. A stronger relationship was established, together with an ongoing interest and practical support between the churches.

4 *Training and celebration*

It is eminently sensible for a strong church to make their training

Colin and Jean White had recommitted their lives to Christ in the early 1980s at West Bridgford Baptist Church. They had not attended church for about twenty years and were both very hungry to learn and grow in Christ. In the following years they studied through the Baptist Union Christian Training Programme. Colin sensed a call to the ministry years earlier and the Holy Spirit began speaking to him again. Whilst continuing to work in a senior position with an industrial company, he studied and trained for the ministry with the Northern Baptist College.

He was placed as student minister at Kegworth Baptist Church, Leicestershire for the last three years of his training. When Colin and Jean took on this responsibility on the Sunday morning worship only mustered between five and ten people, with no evening worship. They committed themselves to the inevitable hard work that was before them. Both have caring gifts and a determination to see fruit from their labour. They began by opening a newly decorated room in the church for Friday morning coffee. This event is still on the programme and has brought many onto the premises and into Sunday worship.

Today, on a Sunday morning, about sixty gather for worship, with twenty to twenty-five of these under the age of twenty-five. Whereas they had to ask for a member from another church to help with the music, they now have their own music group. Mid-week meetings have flourished by comparison with their depressing beginnings — a prayer meeting, youth fellowship, youth club, housegroups and a ladies' meeting. They are now able to sustain an evening service twice a month, which is more traditional in its approach.

available to other local churches. Due to the suspicion sometimes felt, invitations are not always well received. However, when relationship develops no such barrier exists. As well as training, the opportunity to celebrate together becomes a reality. A number of churches hold celebrations on Sunday evenings, and people from such link churches feel very much at home in attending.

FACTORS IN THE RECEIVING CHURCH

A WILLINGNESS TO ADAPT

Jesus said, 'No one pours new wine into old wineskins.' (Luke 5:37) The sad fact is that there are some churches that will not easily be revived. Sometimes attitudes and actions in those who attend are a hindrance to God's work. Such churches may verbalize that they would like help, but it quickly becomes clear that it is only help to maintain 'life as it is'. Any real challenge to the *status quo* meets a brick wall. Frankly, we can waste valuable time trying to help some churches that cannot yet be helped.

In other places, going downhill for so long leads to a new calling upon God, and a readiness to respond to His wishes. I remember sharing with one church that there would be a need to receive the new wine of the Spirit. Their suggestion was that the entire leadership of the church should stand down, so that a group from outside could be imported. This was not the best solution, even though it was a humble and worthy suggestion. The result was that a leader from West Bridgford joined their leadership team. Several years later this particular church is doing very well, and is now helped through the resources of a different church.

WILLINGNESS TO BECOME MATURE

When a church has struggled for decades and has always been the recipient of help, a change of thinking is required. The Holy Spirit wishes every fellowship to grow in faith and confidence, believing that they can be of tremendous significance for the Kingdom of God. The aim of every parent is to encourage their children to become mature and not to continue in dependence.

The receiving church should be encouraged to set goals. If financial help is being provided, decide together how this will be reduced year by year. This is not to be done in a pressured way, but in a way that inspires faith, so that they can rise to meeting more of their own needs. The overall aim is that they should be self-supporting, and possibly become a church that benefits other churches themselves. The helping church should give advice and training on leadership development and a more comprehensive vision. They must allow the church to 'be themselves' and not interfere, but gently encourage them to stand on their own feet.

WILLINGNESS TO MAINTAIN RELATIONSHIP

The Baptist idea of independence has not served our denomination well. Of course, having freedom to exercise local autonomy, where faith and commitment expressed in a local vision can prosper, is valuable. However, a church understands scripture more perfectly when it encourages interdependence. We have truths to learn from the new church streams which practice what they call apostolic and prophetic functions. We may not wish to use this sort of language, as it has connotations that we may find too difficult. Whatever words we choose to use, this type of ministry is legitimate (see Chapter 7).

Our independence bars us from receiving the ongoing godly wisdom from those who could relate to us in the wider Body of Christ. There is real value and safety in a church that has helped another to become strong, not severing the links altogether when the helped church has become self-supporting. This often depends on continuing leadership relationships locally. Inevitably, when church leaders move to another part of the country, the relationship will be harder to sustain.

POSITIVES AND NEGATIVES

Depending on the situation, what is a positive attribute in one church may be a negative one in another. A church that has been part of a community for some years is made up of three factors, either helpful or unhelpful. These are its building, its history and its contacts.

1 BUILDING

A local church's building may have been part of the community for scores, if not hundreds, of years. Even though this is common, it is interesting to note how few church buildings are noticed. When local people are asked, 'Where is a particular church?' they are often not sure. I have discovered this on several occasions when looking for a church where I have been asked to preach.

Kegworth Baptist Church had a building in need of some repair. Extra church financial giving brought a neglected building up to scratch and witnessed to the community that new life was present among them again. In some situations the building can be a hindrance, due to neglect over the years. However, generally speaking, to own your own building is better than not doing so.

2 HISTORY

How does the community perceive the church? One of the main advantages of starting a new church is 'having no baggage'. There are usually some people in the town or village who have had bad experiences of this particular church. For them it is a case of 'Can anything good come out of . . .?' Often the hurts from the past have been in relationship to leaders, and these leaders may have moved on. The fact that the church is known, and certainly isn't a cult, provides a platform on which to repair relationships, restore confidence, and build a new work.

3 CONTACTS

Although some folk rarely go to church, they feel that in some way they belong to one. It may have been where their parents or a relative attended; or they attended a christening, wedding or funeral and felt welcomed. Over the years such churches have built up a considerable number of contacts which can be visited when the church begins its renewal.

The building, history and contacts all add to a church having presence in the community. It takes a new church a long time to create a sense of presence, which is a further reason for trying to resuscitate the old if at all possible.

Since coming to Guildford, I have recognized the need to develop deeper relationships with church leaders and their churches. Guildford has enjoyed good relationships at a leadership level for several years, but of course these can always be deepened. We have received approaches from three churches enquiring about help that Millmead could provide. Two of them were in my first year and we weren't, at that time, in a position to form any strong relationship. Not long ago we were asked for help by a church about ten miles away. We have been providing preachers for some time and recently shared with their members. Our ministry team will take a church weekend with them and begin to form a relationship which, we hope, will be the foundation for closer fellowship in the future.

nine

A DISTRICT STRATEGY

Is it possible for a group of churches to plan together? I have mentioned both the courtesy and the wisdom of noting how churches in your area are planning for evangelism. The genius of DAWN is that there is room for many different expressions of the Body of Christ in the same geographical location, as long as they are not in competition.

In these days of ecumenical conversations and co-operation, denominations have been slower to plant after their own kind for fear of sending the wrong message to the local community. It has been the practice of Councils of Churches to discuss what sort of church should be provided and whether a number of denominations wish to work together. For the last thirty years a growing number of local ecumenical projects (LEP) have developed, with a variety of permutations – Anglican-Methodist, Methodist-URC, Anglican-Baptist-Methodist, etc. One church, but reflecting the different traditions involved. There have been successful LEPs, but sometimes they flounder because there isn't a sufficiently agreed agenda. There can be three different leaders involved (e.g. a curate, part-time Methodist minister, and a lay pastor from another Free Church). However, they work most successfully when the participating churches agree to the appointment of one denominational overall leader.

Although an ecumenical approach appears to be right, because it demonstrates our unity in diversity, I remain to be convinced that it encourages the most fruitful evangelism. Indeed, often the emphasis is firmly placed on the unity of Christians and not on reaching those who are unchurched. Which brings us back to DAWN – recognizing that churches are different, but committed to strong co-operation in planning and strategy to reach the huge harvest. Several towns and cities are discussing district strategies. In Guildford the DAWN movement has been the inspiration, and we are at the very early stages of planning together.

GUILDFORD STRATEGY

The leaders of the district strategy in St Helens, Merseyside were invited to lead a day's conference for the Surrey area. They were asked to explain the DAWN concept and outline the experience of the St Helens' situation. We were told by our speakers that there were four possible levels of co-operation:

- One church has plans for a church planting programme and informs other churches of their intentions.
- Several leaders unite to form a church planting programme and research, pray and plant in consultation.
- Leaders in an area seek to identify and draw together all the evangelical churches to organize a church planting programme.
- Leaders of all churches in an area are encouraged in all phases of a DAWN process for church planting. St Helens is in this category.

As a result of that day, leaders from Guildford met to take the matter further. At this point a number of churches in Guildford had already planted churches, and two or three further plants were in the pipeline. It was accepted that church planting was already taking place in Guildford and this needed to be acknowledged and encouraged.

Church planting is a contentious matter in an interdenominational context. Some church leaders believe that there are already enough churches, and there is sensitivity. about encroaching on another man's 'patch'. This issue is not going to go away, and is more likely to intensify as church planting increases nationwide. One shouldn't underestimate the strength of feeling that will inevitably arise and be expressed amongst a cross-section of church leaders when church planting is on the agenda. It needs to be handled with care.

There are at least two ways to counteract the possible tensions. Firstly, be committed to dialogue and the forming of relationships. Fellow leaders will have less suspicion if we are willing to share ourselves. As we get to know one another more deeply, rather than relying on hearsay, barriers will come down. Secondly, allow the fruit of church planting to speak for itself. Share stories of what is happening in different parts of the country, and focus on the biblical mandate to preach the Gospel to everyone.

During our consultation four of us were asked to form a working group to research the matter — Pete Brayne (new churches), Marion Drew (Salvation Army), Colin Matthews (Church of England) and I. Later, Vic Robertson was asked to join the group to oversee the research into the community. The choice was made on the basis of those who had already given a lead in desiring a district strategy, but also those who were representative of a wider constituency of churches. The working group was charged with the task of drawing up a district strategy likely to be acceptable to a considerable number of churches in the town wards of Guildford — the strategy to include church/congregation planting (although the extent is not yet clear) to fulfil the stated aim of:

the establishment of a church of committed Christians in every community, every neighbourhood, every class and condition of people, where everyone can hear and see demonstrated the Gospel from his own intimates, in his own tongue, and has a reasonable opportunity to become a disciple of Jesus (quote from Donald McGavran, a church growth specialist).

At our first meeting it was obvious that the most important work we could do was to provide two sets of statistics: What was happening in the churches? And, what was happening in the community?

CHURCH CENSUS

On the four Sundays of March each church in the inner wards of Guildford counted numbers of its congregation. This provided more accurate details than the most recent MARC Europe statistics (1989) because thirty-four of the thirty-eight churches took part. The fact that it was part of an overall strategy helped churches to be more co-operative. Also, each member of the working group made personal contact with church leaders, in addition to letters being sent out signed by representatives of the mainline denominations.

In June a half-day conference with church leaders was held to share the findings of the census. At this meeting, the beginnings of a strategy emerged. We looked at different parts of Guildford, and asked the question, 'Are they being adequately evangelized?'

What was the value of the church census? To be honest, there were no great surprises. Most of us were aware of the missing age groups in church and roughly how many people attended on Sunday. However, it was a 'snapshot' of what was happening on a particular Sunday and it did allow us to confirm any trends from previous censuses. It is hoped that we will take an annual or biennial census, so that trends can be observed more closely.

I have shown below a number of graphs with comments,[1] together with a questionnaire which was distributed. The questionnaire that was completed, either on the day or sent to us later, provided helpful information about which parts of Guildford were being evangelized. In theory everywhere should be covered because of parish responsibility. But just because a person lives in a parish, it doesn't mean they are being evangelized. There is much work for us to do in this respect in future discussions. Also, the different sections of society that each church is currently working amongst, or intends to, may form the basis of a town strategy.

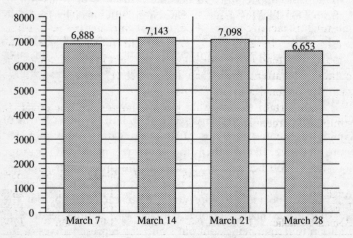

Fig. 1   *Church attendance during March 1993 (from 34 churches)*

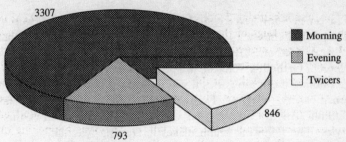

Fig. 2 *Adult attendance — morning and evening*

Churches were asked to count all attenders during the month of March – this being an ideal month (probably the best in the year) as it contains no holidays or particular special church occasions, apart from Mothering Sunday. There was an obvious variance across the Sundays, the most notable being the final Sunday, almost certainly due to the change to British Summer Time. It would seem that losing one hour caused several hundred people to stay in bed on Sunday morning! The average attendance across the Sundays during March was 6,946.

Each participating church was asked to carry out specific analysis of their congregation on the final Sunday in March, from which the following analysis was derived.

The most popular time to attend a church service is in the morning. In fact in Surrey, 34 per cent of churches have a morning service only. In Guildford, 67 per cent of the church-going population attend in the morning, 33 per cent in the evening. The number who attend more than one service (17 per cent) is higher than the national average (14 per cent).

It is important to note that the age ranges are not equal. In summary, percentages are as follows:

| | AGE RANGES | | | | | |
	0–14	15–19	20–29	30–39	40–64	65+
Anglican	11%	4%	7%	14%	38%	26%
Free Church	18%	6%	13%	16%	29%	17%
Roman Catholic	19%	7%	7%	14%	36%	17%

Fig. 3 *Denominational age profile*

The census form asked churches to describe their style of church. They could choose up to three of the following: Anglo-Catholic, Liberal, Catholic, Evangelical, Pentecostal, Charismatic, Low Church, Orthodox, Radical, or specify a description of their own. Examining these categories it was discovered that there were two broad styles, that of Evangelical (seventeen churches) and Catholic/Anglo-Catholic (ten churches), leaving seven 'Other' styles. The following graph makes interesting reading:

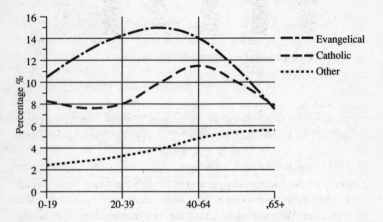

Fig. 4 *Church styles and age groups as a percentage of all church attenders*

The age ranges are more evenly spread than on the previous graph. Also, the percentage is that of all church attenders (i.e. 8 per cent of all church attenders were aged under twenty and of a Catholic style).

Comparing the age profile of the church with that of the town makes interesting reading. From the statistics gathered, it is clear that amongst church attenders there is a much higher proportion of women than men. But also, as this graph shows, there is a much higher proportion of older people.

An interesting exercise is to forecast what attendance we can expect in twenty years' time, bearing in mind a dramatically dropping child attendance. In addition, the Office of Population and Censuses advises that the number of people aged between fifteen and twenty-nine will reduce up to the year 2000. 'This is particularly important as

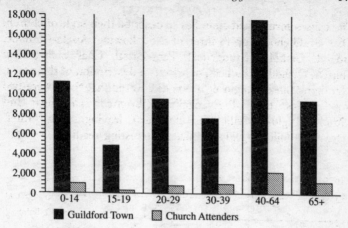

Fig. 5 *Age of church attenders against town population*

many get their experience of church leadership in these years,' reports Peter Brierley in the book *Act on the Facts*.[2]

COMMUNITY SURVEY

A survey of the community proved to be more of a headache. What were the right questions, and how were we to collect the information? We wanted to know the answers to these questions:

- How much do the community know about the churches?
- How much do they know about the Christian message?
- What is the spiritual climate like?
- How much desire is there for spiritual experience, and especially of Christianity?
- What are the bridges that can be built into the community?

How not to do it!

We organized a pilot group so that we could work out the best questions for a future questionnaire. We sent out 150 letters at random, explaining what we were hoping to do, and enclosing a reply paid postcard. If they regularly attended church we should like the information, but we were really inviting those with no church contact to a meeting.

GUILDFORD CHURCH CENSUS

Geographical Evangelism

1 Is there an area of the town that your church feels responsible to evangelize? (YES/NO)

   If 'YES', please shade the area on the map, *and* indicate how this is being carried out by ticking the boxes below, adding any comments to the right:–

   ☐ Literature through doors _____
   ☐ Door-to-door visiting _____
   ☐ Strong friendship evangelism emphasis _____
   ☐ Walks of witness _____
   ☐ Prayer walks _____
   ☐ Events/Programmes provided for area _____
   _____
   _____
   OTHER _____
   _____

2 Is there a more specific geographical focus for your evangelism other than (1) above? (YES/NO)

   If 'YES', please describe that area: _____
   _____

Specific Group Evangelism

3 Which sections of society would you expect your church style and structure equips you to reach best? For example:– professionals, single adults, retired, youth, disadvantaged, young families, etc.
   _____
   _____
   _____

4 Are there any specific programmes that you currently run which are targeted towards particular groups? Please indicate whether these are Church Programmes (C), or individuals' involvement (I).

   ☐ Mother & Toddlers (C/I) _____
   ☐ Overseas students (C/I) _____
   ☐ Youth in community (C/I) _____
   ☐ Children in community (C/I) _____
   ☐ Business people (C/I) _____
   ☐ Retired (C/I) _____

Fig. 6 *Questionnaire used in Guildford District Strategy Church Census*

☐ Singles (C/I) _____
☐ Single-parent families (C/I) _____
☐ Schools work (C/I) _____
OTHER _____
_____
_____
_____

Social Action

5 In what areas does your church provide a social service in the community? Please indicate whether these are Church Programmes (C), or individuals' involvement (I).

☐ Hospital visiting (C/I) _____
☐ Mental Illness (C/I) _____
☐ Physical disability (C/I) _____
☐ Homeless (C/I) _____
☐ Unemployed (C/I) _____
☐ School support (C/I) _____
☐ Learning difficulties (C/I) _____
☐ HIV/Aids (C/I) _____
☐ Alcohol abuse (C/I) _____
☐ Drug dependancy (C/I) _____
☐ Legal advice (C/I) _____
☐ Home pastoral visiting (C/I) _____

Specialist Counselling (tick as appropriate)

☐ Bereavement (C/I) _____
☐ Marriage preparation (C/I) _____
☐ Marriage counselling (C/I) _____
☐ Divorcees (C/I) _____
☐ Family counselling (C/I) _____
☐ Depression (C/I) _____
☐ Eating disorders (C/I) _____
☐ Debt counselling (C/I) _____
OTHER _____
_____
_____
_____

Name _____

Church _____

Your role in the Church _____

QUESTIONNAIRE   No. _____   YES   NO

1. Do you personally believe a religious faith is important in life? ☐ ☐

2. Do you regularly attend a church or religious meeting? ☐ ☐

3. If 'No', have you ever regularly attended church? ☐ ☐

4. When did you stop going?   Year _____

5. Why did you stop going?
   (a) Unfriendly ☐   (b) Irrelevant ☐   (c) Hurt ☐
   (d) Boring ☐   (e) Poor teaching ☐   (f) Other ☐

6. Do other members of this household attend a church? ☐ ☐

7. Did anyone else in your family attend a church? ☐ ☐

8. Did you go to Sunday School?
   (a) Regularly ☐   (b) Occasionally ☐   (c) Never ☐

9. Has anyone ever invited you to a church service? (not mailed literature) ☐ ☐

10. Do you have a friend who attends a church regularly? ☐ ☐

11. Which is your local church? _____

12. What is your impression of it?
    (a) Friendly ☐   (b) Unfriendly ☐   (c) Other _____

13. If all the churches closed, would it matter? ☐ ☐

14. Which best describes your belief?
    (a) Christian ☐   (b) Undecided ☐   (c) Other _____

15. Do you believe there is a God? ☐ ☐

16. Do you believe Jesus Christ ever existed? ☐ ☐

Fig. 7   *Questionnaire used in Guildford District Strategy Area Survey*

17. Do you believe Jesus Christ was raised from
the dead? ☐ ☐

18. If 'Yes', does it matter to you? Answer in range 1 - 5
(where 1 = not at all and 5 = extremely)
1 ☐   2 ☐   3 ☐   4 ☐   5 ☐

19. Is the Bible relevant for life today? ☐ ☐

20. If so, in what way? _____

21. Sex   Male ☐   Female ☐

22. (a) Under 18 ☐ (b) 18-29 ☐ (c) 30-39 ☐ (d) 40-59 ☐
(e) Over 60 ☐

23. At what age did you complete full-time education? _____

24. Married ☐ Single ☐ Widow/widower ☐ Divorced ☐ Other ☐

25. Number of children living at home (by age)
Under 5 ☐ 6-10 ☐ 11-16 ☐ Over 16 ☐

26. Number of years at present address _____

27. Would you like to talk to someone about Christianity? ☐ ☐

If 'Yes'   Name _____

Address _____

Postcode _____

'Thank you for giving us your time.'

Name of Interviewer _____

Ward _____

We discovered that church-goers were willing to send in their information. Interestingly, from such a small sample, it confirmed the MARC Europe percentage for those who attended church in Guildford (12 per cent in 1989). However, only three people were willing to attend an evening meeting to share their opinions. We concluded that postal research is not effective.

Plan B

It was decided to go to fifty homes at random to check out a questionnaire which would form the basis of one that would be used with 1,000 people. This proved more successful. On the whole, folk were willing to answer the questions, and conversations developed further.

After refinement, a revised questionnaire was used. Each home received a letter beforehand, explaining that two people would be calling to see them on behalf of the Guildford churches. We trained about a hundred people (to work in pairs), from a mixture of churches. Each pair visited twenty pre-selected homes, covering the inner wards of Guildford. Training was not complicated – mainly practical advice on how to handle the interview.

It would entail far too much information to publish the results of the community survey. The following[3] are some of the general conclusions from 500 of the overall sample.

Nearly 200 people either declined to answer the questions or were out after a second visit. A high percentage of them were in particular parts of Guildford, which either indicates that these are harder areas to penetrate, or that the people were suspicious of what might be considered a middle-class approach. (A letter was sent beforehand, and in these more unresponsive areas a better response was gained through 'cold visiting', i.e. without the preparation letter.)

Those not wishing to answer are likely to be people less interested, and so the statistics that follow need to take this into account. We are dealing, therefore, with about 300 replies.

- 227 believed that a personal religious faith was important in life, but only 78 of these said that they attended a church or religious meeting.

- Why did people stop attending church? The five categories that we suggested scored quite low ('irrelevant' and 'boring' being the most frequently listed), but 116 people gave other reasons. The main ones were 'moving house', 'family commitments' and 'being too busy'.

- We were encouraged to discover that 197 had a friend who attended church regularly, although 99 did not. As relationships are the main way in which people are introduced to the Christian faith, it reinforces the need to develop meaningful contact with people.

- 223 believed that it would matter if all the churches closed (69 thought it would not). There is obviously a belief that the Church has an important role to play, even if folk are not wanting to 'sign up'.

- A high proportion described themselves as Christian – 234 – with 36 being undecided, and 35 'other'. We have known for a long time that there is considerable confusion in the mind of the community on this subject, but it was surprising to see such a large number who still wished to be identified with this label.

- We knew that there was widespread belief in God, but wanted to know what people's beliefs were about Jesus Christ's existence and His resurrection. 263 believed that Jesus Christ existed (20 did not), and 179 believed that He rose from the dead (78 did not, and 36 were unsure). As to whether it mattered to them (on a scale of 1-5), the results were: Scale 1: 28; 2: 17; 3: 42; 4: 22; and 5: 83.

- We can usually convince a thinking person that Jesus Christ existed, as it is historical fact, but the very high number who believe He rose from the dead surprised me. Although of these only about a hundred thought it mattered to them.

- Similarly, 217 believed that the Bible was relevant for life today, 74 did not. When we asked in what way it was relevant, the main reasons given were 'a moral code' and 'teaching on how to live'. Hardly any spoke of it as being God's word, or of Jesus Christ.

- The final question concerned whether they would like to talk further about Christianity. From this first sample, eight responded affirmatively.

The working group, and then church leaders, will have to scrutinize the final results closely. But it is clear that the Church has failed to communicate the message of Christianity when such high numbers will assent to basic Christian doctrines, but not translate them into a Christian lifestyle.

So is a district strategy possible? It is going to take considerable time to share with all the church leaders, and it isn't at all clear yet how many churches are going to 'own' a strategy. We don't know at which level of co-operation we are going to be able to operate (see district strategy in Merseyside points). There will certainly be co-operation between a number of churches because this is already happening.

We were encouraged recently with the points made by Chris Forster, DAWN Co-ordinator, who said that for a district strategy to be successful, four ingredients are necessary. These are: corporate prayer, research, a commitment to church planting, and local training in evangelism. With the recent decision of a number of Guildford churches to start a training school in evangelism, we believe the fourth ingredient has now been put in place.

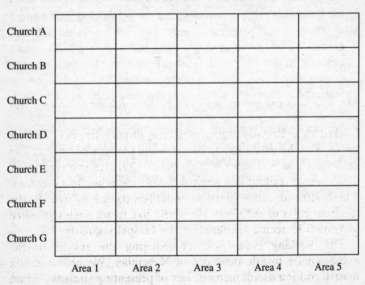

Fig. 8   *Matrix grid showing which churches cover different geographical areas*

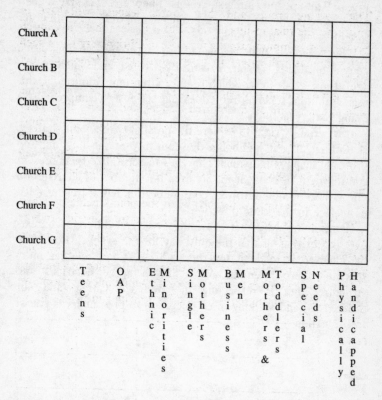

Fig. 9 *Matrix grid showing which churches cover different population groups*

I asked Pete Brayne, chairman of the district strategy working group, what he would like to see. He reminded me of a vision that he believed he was given in September 1991. He saw streams of living water coming out from different churches in Guildford. These streams came together and then parted to irrigate the different parts of the town. He would like to see each individual of Guildford seeing and hearing the Gospel regularly.

The working group will be bringing the results of the questionnaire to a leaders' day in November. We believe that a matrix grid is a useful pictorial way of presenting strategy. Figure 8 shows the evangelization task divided into geographical, and

Figure 9 into people/interest, groups. There are, of course, a great many more people and interest groups to add to Figure 9 in order to gain a complete picture.

This exercise will enable us to ascertain whether each geographical area is being realistically covered, and which are the age/ethnic groups etc, which require attention. Admittedly, this is an ambitious scheme, but it does take seriously a comprehensive evangelistic vision.

It is certainly right to explore the possibility of a joint strategy. If nothing else, it highlights the enormity of the mission, and probably inspires individual churches to scrutinize their present commitment to evangelism. So, even if a number of churches do not wish to become involved, communication has at least enabled us to face in the same direction.

A prophetic word that has come in several different contexts over recent years is that the only way for the evangelistic task to be achieved is to do it together. This isn't just another unity scheme where attempts are made to agree doctrines and structures, but is respecting the Body of Christ (and our differences) and working in co-operation to present Jesus Christ to the nation.

'IT CAN'T HAPPEN IN OUR CHURCH!'

You may be convinced that new churches should be planted, but you cannot believe that your own church can be involved. The obstacles are too large so you are tempted to leave it to others. Are the hurdles as formidable as you think? A church may not be planted by you for several years, and now is the time to plan.

NEGATIVES AND POSITIVES OF PLANTING

There are ten reasons given by church leaders and members for not embarking on a planting vision. However, there are many strong arguments in favour of planting.

1 WE'RE NOT LARGE ENOUGH

Most churches believe that they have to be relatively large (200–300 members) before they can contemplate sponsoring another church. But how large is large enough? This is a hard question to answer because the number is affected by the depth of evangelistic vision, attitude in the members, and the level of maturity of a church.

In other countries, such as Brazil, where the climate of church growth is very different, new churches are planted from quite a small base. A couple of families might move to another town and together plant a church. In this sort of plant the mother church is not affected greatly by the loss. However, this is a country where the spiritual soil is very fertile and where faith and commitment are high.

New churches have begun in the UK with a dedicated couple or a small team. In the 1970s, Lewis and Molly Misselbrooke began a new church on the Chelmsley Wood estate near Birmingham, which today has its own building. Other churches which do not have sufficient people none the less release those who are available and plant the seed which will grow into a larger plant.

Rochdale

The Methodist circuit at Rochdale has begun new works with limited resources, as planting has been more in response to opportunity and need rather than a carefully planned strategy. The plant at Wallbank, an older council estate, came about through God moving among the people of Whitworth Methodist Church. The number of Christians grew and, when they had to sell their old and decrepit building, they moved their church into a baker's shop and adjoining house on the main street of Whitworth. As well as a place of worship, it became a drop-in centre, and a programme with children and young people developed. Because of this involvement they were asked by the county council to take over the running of a family centre on Wallbank housing estate three-quarters of a mile away. The church agreed and, with staff salaries and a building supplied, they began to hold play groups and after-school clubs. These gave them the opportunity to develop relationships with the local people.

Last year they began to hold short, informal services on Sunday afternoons at the centre. To date they have attracted mainly children with just a few adults. This plant is dependent on local Christians becoming involved, as the mother church is itself at full stretch without supporting a new congregation.

The Belfield plant came out of one man's prayer following his conversion at Thrum Hall Methodist Church. When he started working as a care assistant on the Belfield estate, God began to give him a vision of a visible Christian witness there, using the newly built community centre. Several members of Thrum Hall, together with other local Christians, began to hold a series of evening celebrations, following door-to-door visiting and leaflet distribution. Again, this work attracted a great many children but relatively few adults. However, there were commitments to Christ and a nurture group was established, meeting weekly in a home.

Out of this they have begun an afternoon Sunday School and are continuing their monthly celebrations. They held a week of mission and hope to open the Sunday afternoon event to adults and increase the numbers attending the nurture group. In just eighteen months, from an initial Gospel concert, they have planted a Christian witness, with the strong possibility of establishing a congregation on Belfield estate. They have all the right ingredients to grow — vision, prayer, churches working together, leadership being released, venue, and a children's programme already in progress.

Guildford

In Guildford the Community Church believed that it was right to plant in the Stoke Road area. They had successfully planted a church in Park Barn and so looked for willing members to get this second venture off the ground. After several months it became clear that the number of adults who were committed was only thirteen. The leader of the group was convinced that this should not be seen as a set-back. He shared the following points with those concerned:

- We will obviously have to proceed differently, as forty-two adults founded Park Barn compared with thirteen at Stoke.
- We will have to lean more heavily on the sending church for resources.
- We need to forget about the actual timing of the plant as it was initially envisaged, so that we can get on with loving and caring for the people who live in the Stoke area.
- The people who become Christians as a result of our outreach will be taken to the mother church on Sundays, but mid-week meetings will be held in Stoke, emphasizing our commitment to the community.
- These provide the steps to planting a church in Stoke Road, and so it is essential that we give emphasis to reaching the unchurched.

Many churches could release ten or more members to evangelize in a community as a preparation for a church plant, especially if they have strong encouragement and resources from their mother church.

2 THERE IS NO ADEQUATE BUILDING

In my early days I believed there was no real problem in finding a building to rent. I now realize that in some places this is not the case. Also, if you adopt a multi-congregational model, there may not be a large enough and suitable building to house all the congregations. You may have to broaden people's outlook as to what qualifies as a place of worship. If members are basing their decision on a similar building to the church sanctuary, they will reject certain venues as 'unholy'.

When looking for a venue for one of the Nottingham congregations we were trying to decide whether or not to use the Dancing Slipper. The owner would allow the church to use the night club, but for a variety of reasons it was not suitable. The alcohol consumed on the previous evening and the smoky atmosphere meant that the smell could have been hard to remove by early Sunday morning. According to the New Testament, it is the people of God who are holy, not buildings. There are strong arguments for worshipping in a building where the world regularly meets – it sharpens up our sense of mission, although we may have to pray for its spiritual cleansing every time we use it.

Clearly some buildings are more conducive to worship than others. Spend time finding the most appropriate one, but recognize that almost anywhere is possible if it meets your needs. In Kensington Temple's manual for their satellite churches, they provide the following list of possible venues:

- Seventh Day Adventists tend not to use Sundays
- Cinema
- Shop front
- Church hall
- Scouts or other organizations' halls
- Dance hall
- Porta-cabin
- Political party hall
- Denominational church
- Factory building
- School (public and private)
- Working men's club
- Tennis or golf club house
- Community centre
- Hotel room
- Library

- YMCA
- Restaurants
- Housing estate halls
- Your own house

- Synagogue
- Public houses
- Swimming baths

3 WE DON'T HAVE A LEADER

The leader is crucial, so wait until the person is provided. This underlines the necessity for long-term planning. Not everything can happen at once, so plan ahead for it. This may involve sending a potential leader on a training course. These vary in length and in depth of theological content (see Appendix A).

If there isn't a suitable person in the church then employ another member of staff, if finances are available. In Guildford, having looked in our membership for a person to set aside full-time for church planting, we decided to employ from outside. Alternatively, if there is strong conviction within the church that planting churches is right, encourage specific prayer. God may send the planter from another fellowship or move him/her into the area.

4 THE CHURCH IS NOT IN FAVOUR OF IT

This situation prevails in many churches. Church planting will affect the whole of the church and members sense this potential upheaval when the matter is raised. Also, many will not be at all convinced that it is the right direction in which to move. It will take time to bring the church to a position of being in favour. It is not simply a matter of changing people's minds, but bringing about a change in the spiritual climate. At the heart of the matter is vision. But how do you receive and communicate vision which results in the membership embracing church planting?

I have explained how the churches in Nottingham and Guildford received and shared the vision with the church membership in Chapter 1. The following points are also pertinent:

Vision comes from God

Usually, through a leader's relationship with God a sense of direction is planted within him. The leader will need to be a student of scripture because this provides the background to God's nature and ways. Vision may begin with an idea, but it comes with faith and a sense of excitement. At this stage it may not be easy to articulate – you only have a 'spiritual hunch' that you are thinking in the right direction.

If the vision is centred in a verse or passage of scripture it carries its own 'spiritual weight' and significance. It also enables people to accept it more easily. There were two passages of scripture which were particularly inspiring during the years at Nottingham: Ephesians 4:11–13 and Isaiah 54:2–3. I used to remind the people of them periodically as foundation points for the vision. Ephesians 4 explains that every member is 'in the ministry'. The role of leadership is to prepare and train those in the church for Christian service. This is fundamental to a growing church and maximizes the amount of Christian service that is available to church and community. The challenge of Isaiah 54 is to extend the tent in which you live. This is done by enlarging the geographical vision and digging deeper foundations ('lengthen your cords and strengthen your stakes') so that a more extensive work can be sustained. We were particularly struck by the language of empty towns and cities being filled with people. We understood this as a mandate to reach out further into the surrounding villages, and to work and pray for spiritual life to flood these communities.

Confirmed by others

As a person with vision begins to share what he believes is the best way forward, he receives encouragement. What the 'visionary' thinks is of no particular significance, others may begin to respond to the vision expressed with a new sense of revelation. Of course, it may be that other people take no interest in what is being shared – which may indicate that it isn't vision at all; or that it is too early to share it, its day has not yet come. Leaders should not be afraid to wait for the confirmation of godly people as there is safety in this.

Submit to God

It is wise to submit these initial thoughts to God for further confirmation. Vision develops over a period of time and we need not fear, at this stage, that we might 'miss the boat'. If it is only a good idea, rather than a 'God idea', it will lose its power in your mind and heart. However, if the Lord is speaking, He will be prompting you to take it further.

Overcoming reluctance

Most, if not all, biblical characters were reluctant when they were asked to embark on a new enterprise for the Lord. Moses is the classic case of a man coming up with five different reasons why he was the wrong choice (Exodus 3–4). This reluctance is natural and healthy but must be overcome. Any vision worth its salt will not be implemented easily. It will require encouragement from the Holy Spirit, and leaders to set it in place.

Express it clearly

An indispensable element is the ability to communicate vision. You will not motivate the hearts of church members if they do not understand what is in your heart. Spend time committing your thoughts to paper and expressing them simply, emphasizing the main points. At this stage it has entered the forum of the church, and through teaching and encouragement the vision will gradually be owned by them.

5 WE DON'T HAVE THE FINANCE

If a vision for church planting has emerged, lack of finance should not be allowed to dictate. The most 'successful' churches and movements have not had the money when the vision was first embarked upon. I often reflect, and wonder, how some movements can employ scores of people, purchase land, build premises and give to the poor. If there is vision from God in a church's heart, money will be found.

Don't overlook other sources of finance. Denominations need challenging to use their resources for adventurous new enterprises. Also local trusts, who have the monies set aside for the spread of the Gospel, can be asked. Considerable finance is available through church members. It is often the vision and commitment to a demanding new work that releases new levels of finance to sustain it.

6 IS IT THE RIGHT TIME?

Timing is important and the Holy Spirit will give clarity on this point as He is invited into the centre of your plans. Church planting is an urgent work, but God is prepared to wait for the most opportune time. The people and the situation need to be prepared. In Nottingham we tried to plant congregations too quickly and stretched the resources of the mother. There may be a delay of several years until God gives the green light. The long-term plan is to plant, but there are other ways in which the Lord will continue to use the church in the meantime.

Adrian Argile, minister of Leyland Baptist Church, Lancashire, has been convinced about the need to plant new churches since his college days at Spurgeons. The village of Euxton, about four miles from them, was proposed as a possible planting area. Very quickly a housegroup began in the village, most of whom lived in Euxton. Members of the church were asked who would be willing to commit themselves: they had been kept informed throughout, so it wasn't a new idea. Only twelve people were willing. This was clearly not the right time. Why?

- The door-to-door visiting had not resulted in much response.
- Those wanting to be involved needed to demonstrate greater evangelistic commitment.
- The Governors of the local school in Euxton, who had earlier indicated their willingness to rent, changed their minds.

Adrian recognized that the Holy Spirit was causing them to reconsider the timing of the church plant. It was a natural halt, and it should not be rushed.

Interestingly, at about the same time, another outreach possibility opened out. Three-quarters of a mile from Leyland is a community of 1,500 people on an estate called Wade Hall. A shop had been empty for two years and was being offered to the church by the council. They quickly cleared a change of use with the council so that it could function as a community centre. The church's desire is to appoint a community worker. Adrian believes that eventually this will lead to establishing a congregation in this community. He also expects that a congregation will be planted in Euxton, but only when the spiritual conditions are favourable.

7 ANOTHER CHURCH WANTS TO PLANT IN THE SAME AREA

It is imperative to be aware of the church planting intentions of all the local churches. If fellow leaders have been consulted in the way described in Chapter 1, there should be no confusion. However, if in initial research it is discovered that another church has plans and is well down the road with its preparation, it may be right to bow out graciously. Endorse their work and give encouragement.

If both churches are at early stages in their plans, a more comprehensive discussion needs to take place. There are a number of questions to consider. Could resources be shared? Do the prospective churches share a similar ethos and approach to ministry? It does not follow that planting together will come easily, but it should be explored. What is the population in the proposed area? Is there room for two new churches? If a community has 15,000 people and only a couple of churches serving them, according to the DAWN principle there is plenty of room for two or more churches serving Christ 'after their own kind'. The keys to this are humility and respecting the Body of Christ.

8 WE DON'T MIND TRAVELLING, SO WHY PLANT IN THE NEIGHBOURHOOD?

This comment reflects the church-going habits of thousands in this country. In all the concentration on neighbourhood evangelism, we must not lose sight of the ministry of churches that draw folk from a large geographical area. Some are going to be won to Christ from a church on their doorstep. Others are going to be attracted by large numbers and the inspiration and stimulus of outstanding teaching and worship. It follows, therefore, that there are many who will *not* travel a distance to church, and will only respond to Christ within their culture and community. We must not deceive ourselves that high mobility will cater for everyone's needs.

9 WE DON'T HAVE ANY PEOPLE LIVING IN THE PROPOSED AREA

This is quite common. There are either no members who live in the community or possibly just one family. A particular community might have been in the minds of a church for several years, but no one is joining the church from that area. If planting in this community is more than simply a good idea (i.e. the church has a conviction that God is pointing in this direction), then radical thinking and action is called for. The only way a church will be planted is if individuals give the time and commitment to it.

The church can be challenged to invite members to move house in order to live in the vicinity. This is the practice of Pioneer People, who have seen the need to encourage their members to uproot and move. If a strong core group can be created through this strategy, it can be added to by those who travel into the area. Clearly, this approach requires strong commitment, which is why the church needs to have done its homework in knowing God's leading. If folk demonstrate their commitment by being willing to move house, there should be less worry about their level of commitment to planting a church.

10 EVANGELICAL CHURCHES HAVE NEVER SUCCEEDED IN THAT AREA

There are some who believe that there is no such thing as a hard area to penetrate with the Gospel – they are all equally hard. Certainly we can excuse ourselves by describing particular villages, towns, etc. as especially resistant to the Gospel. It may be that we haven't tried hard enough. If recent teaching about spiritual warfare is to be believed, certain geographical communities are 'more in Satan's grip' than others. I am persuaded that this is the case, but I also believe that it should not deter us.

If so-called 'hard' areas have been left alone because the Church has failed there in the past, what does this say about our belief in the Christian Gospel? Going everywhere to preach the Gospel includes all the hard areas. Jesus demonstrated this by His life, and has left sufficient teaching for us to know that 'the works of darkness are subject' to Him (Luke 10:18–20). It will require considerable prayer preparation and strong proclamation of the message of Christ's Lordship. Rightly understood, church planting is about spiritual warfare because it is unashamedly reclaiming ground from our enemy. It is simply that certain areas may be more demanding in this respect.

Other cultures as well

One hugely neglected area is that of ethnic minorities and greater penetration into sub-cultures and what are sometimes called 'working-class communities'. Stuart Murray, Director of the Church Planting Course at Spurgeons College, argues that we are not developing different churches, we are largely planting clones of ourselves. This is certainly true. Most of the church planting done is not crossing cultures, but planting in communities where folk are culturally similar. He gives four main reasons for this:

- *Location:* If planting a church near to itself, very little thought is given to planting a different sort of church.
- *Motivation:* If the new church is being planted because the mother church is full, again very little thought may be given to planting anything radically different.
- *Personnel:* If those doing the planting are dependent on the insight of mother church leadership, there is also less likelihood of a significantly different new church emerging.
- *Structure:* If those who are planting are only concerned about more churches, they will not apply their minds to the type of churches that need planting.

Stuart writes, 'Denominational loyalty, doctrinal convictions, trusted traditions, and the daunting challenge of ecclesiological renewal, all tend to inhibit the asking of radical questions. It is enough to gear up to plant a new church without raising controversial questions about the nature of the church.'[1] There is a desperate need for us to plant churches that are relevant to the particular culture. It is beginning to happen with youth churches, ethnic churches and churches for the unchurched, but much more time, commitment, and boldness are called for.

MOTIVATION

Those who take up the challenges of church planting need some kind of motivation. For me, there are four motivating factors which help me to remain committed to church planting.

1 GOD IS EMPHASIZING MISSION

This could be considered a trite statement. Hasn't God always been committed to reaching the world that He created and drawing us back to Himself? The answer must be 'Yes'. We have the commands of scripture to love, to go, to preach, to fight against Satan and sin, to work until the Gospel is taken to all the nations. These commands in themselves are sufficient to motivate evangelism.

However, I wonder if there is an even greater highlighting of mission in our day. There is no question that the Holy Spirit is being poured out in every continent, and this is resulting in conversions and church planting. If we are listening to 'what the Spirit is saying to the churches', we will discover a new sense of mission rising within us.

2 ENOUGH WORK FOR EVERYONE

I believe church leadership is about enabling church members to 'do the work of ministry', so-called 'every-member ministry'. Many more of God's people can be encouraged to serve Him evangelistically and find their place within the Body of Christ. What is the point of just a few doing all the work? Common sense tells us that if the load is shared, far more can be achieved.

Church planting sets Christians apart to serve the Lord in new ways. They certainly don't feel adequate for the task initially, but it has the effect of stimulating spiritual growth. If I can encourage other Christians to give time and training to the great commission, I am a happy man. How are we going to reach the millions who are not yet aware of His love, if thousands more of us do not become actively involved? The Holy Spirit has set His agenda, let us fulfil it.

3 DON'T HOLD BACK

Whilst looking at Isaiah 54:2–3 – the verses that inspired church planting in Nottingham – I noticed the phrase 'do not hold back'. This was a time of hesitation: we had begun to plant, and inevitably questions arise in a leader's mind. I am cautious by nature and so did not want to rush the next stage. I heard God speak through these four words – it was right to keep going forward. The Holy Spirit gives boldness to those of us who are tempted to be hesitant and hold back. I have tried to make this a spiritual principle in my life. 'Holding back' is about doubt, which can lead to disabling the church. Of course, there is a right spiritual hesitancy which is an aspect of wisdom. However, too many of us hold back when we should be going forward. The work will only get done *if we do it*.

4 PEOPLE'S ENCOURAGEMENT

I have made my fair share of mistakes, and have been so grateful to those who believed in me none the less. These mistakes included timing, choices of people, poor communication, not thinking plans through sufficiently, not being supportive enough after delegating . . . it could be a long list. A marvellous discovery that I made as a church leader was that people are willing to stand by you when 'everything hasn't gone quite right'. Members of West Bridgford Baptist Church and the Millmead Centre have demonstrated this with their love and encouragement. This leads to strong motivation. It means that I can keep leading the people into church planting even if I don't get everything exactly right. The truth is that none of us ever will.

Can I encourage you to plant churches?

TRAINING THE LEADER

CHURCH PLANTING COURSES

DITCHDIGGERS

Based in Reading, Berkshire this is a full-time course lasting one year, run by the local network of churches. Studies include a full Bible survey and teaching on major doctrines. Practical studies take in leadership training, evangelism and church planting, among others. After the initial six weeks, students will gain practical experience by being involved in either a church planting team in Reading, a street evangelism team, or in schools presentation. Ten days of the year will be spent on mission abroad.

Further information from:
Ditchdiggers, 34a Hilltop Road, Earley, Reading, Berkshire RG6 1DB
Telephone: 0734 262003

G.E.T.GOING

Guildford Evangelism Training programme is based in Guildford, Surrey and run by a group of local churches. The one-year, full-time course offers four modules: discipleship, Bible teaching, missions, and the Church. Students will gain understanding of church planting both from the teaching and also from practical experience, with placements in churches in and around Guildford. A part-time course is also available.

Further information from:
G.E.T.Going, 14/15 Queen's Road, Guildford, Surrey GU1 4JJ
Telephone: 0483 571180

ICHTHUS TRAINING PROGRAMME

Ichthus have a number of study options under their programme:

Network is for those with leadership gifts, wanting to enter full-time Christian work. The course lasts one year from January to December. Minimum age is twenty-three. Networkers will develop skills in a number of areas including leadership, pioneer evangelism, and church planting. The programme covers biblical teaching, practical church planting and outside missions.

Fieldwork, a training programme based in the Middle East, is for those with a clear sense of calling to be pioneers in evangelism and church planting in the Muslim world.

Groundwork provides short-term training and involvement in practical evangelism with experience of front line church plants. The course lasts for ten weeks from June to August. Minimum age is eighteen.

Summer Project is a short course of two or four weeks and includes a teaching programme, together with sessions of practical evangelism.

Further information from:
The Training Administrator, Ichthus Christian Fellowship,
107 Stanstead Road, Forest Hill, London SE23 1HH
Telephone: 081 291 4057

INTERNATIONAL BIBLE INSTITUTE OF LONDON

Based at Kensington Temple, the Institute run a number of courses including the Diploma of Christian Studies. This is a one-year course on a broad-based curriculum, training both existing and future leaders. Aspects of church planting are covered within the syllabus. Students are expected to participate in areas of practical ministry, either in Kensington Temple or in their own church. There are also a number of part-time courses available.

Further information from:
International Bible Institute of London, Kensington Temple,
Kensington Park Road, Notting Hall Gate, London W11 3BY
Telephone: 071 727 4877 or 071 229 5630

MOORLANDS COLLEGE

The Church Planting Course has been established, in partnership with Yeovil Community Church, for those who are unable to follow a full Bible college course. It gives specific input in those areas seen as essential for undertaking a church planting ministry, but is not a substitute for existing courses for pastoral leadership. It runs for ten months from the middle of September, with half of each week at Moorlands and half in placement at Yeovil Community Church.

Further information from:
Dave Edwins, Moorlands College, Sopley, Christchurch,
Dorset BH23 7AT
Telephone: 0425 72369

OASIS/SPURGEONS COLLEGE

The Church Planting and Evangelism Course lasts three years. Students attend college one day a week during each term. The rest of the time is spent in practical training in a church placement, with home study and further tuition leading to other qualifications. The placement can be in the student's home church. This course is also a recognized route towards the Baptist ministry.

Further information from:
Stuart Murray, Oasis Director of Church Planting and Evangelism,
Spurgeons College, 189 South Norwood Hill, London SE25 6DJ
Telephone: 081 653 0850

YOUTH WITH A MISSION

The School of Church Planting and Ministry run by YWAM lasts four months, with placement options following. The course is designed for lay leaders, ministry leaders, church planters, pastors, and those working alongside local churches in para-church organizations. The first fourteen weeks is a lecture phase in St Helens with some practical ministry in local churches. Phase Two places students in short-term outreach or longer-term placements. These can be from three months to two years, depending on individual choice.

Further information from:
Youth With A Mission, Parr Mount School, Sorogold Street,
Parr Mount, St Helens, Merseyside WA9 1AX
Telephone: 0744 24786

ORIGINAL MATERIAL

THE PEARLY GATES HURDLES

Characters: Peter and Julian, television racing commentators
Five runners: The Bishop, Do Gooder, The Rich Man, Mere
Professor and The Novice

PETER: *(Unseen, speaking through a microphone and loudspeaker.)*
Good morning and welcome to the first race of the day here
at the Millmead course in Guildford, the 11.20. We're looking
forward to a good day's racing here at this pleasant course on
the banks of the Wey. Always a popular venue, there's a good
crowd here already for the first race, something of a Millmead
classic this, the Pearly Gates Hurdles. Run over a mile and seven
furlongs, over eight flights, it's open to all comers. Julian has
been down in the paddock and has the latest prices.

JULIAN: *(Enters with microphone.)* Thank you Peter. Yes, as Peter
says, something of a classic this and I think we're in for a good
race today. Not an easy course this to forecast a winner on, but
there's no doubt who the favourite is today. Looking every inch
a winner, as if he's already one of St Peter's buddies, at 5–4 on
is The Bishop.

*(Enter The Bishop, who parades around while Julian is describing
him before taking up a position facing the congregation. The other
runners do likewise in their turn.)*

Dressing down a little for the occasion today, but still very
impressive, this runner by Tradition out of the Upper House
has a lot of support.

Next to The Bishop is Do Gooder, a very familiar sight at
hospitals and prisons around the country, stalwart of the WRVS

and Meals On Wheels. A very effective filly this, perhaps more efficient than attractive, can be a trifle overbearing. At 8–1 in from 14–1 since yesterday, she could well provide something of an upset today. She's certainly a very energetic and well-intentioned runner, if a little undisciplined.

Lack of discipline is certainly a criticism that can't be levied at our third runner, The Rich Man. Almost pedantically methodical and thorough, he wouldn't have got where he is without it. By Hard Graft out of Filthy Lucre he comes from a long line of winners. A great-grandson of Philanthropy, there's a streak of that illustrious forebear in him. But he is carrying the heaviest weight this morning and that could count against him. Ideally suited to very hard going, he could be at something of a disadvantage today and that's reflected in the pricing at 20–1 out from 14–1.

This morning's second favourite at 3–1 is certainly the most spectacular when in full flight, with that distinctive long flowing mane. Mere Professor shares certain characteristics with the favourite but with greater erudition. One of two local runners, trained on the slopes of Stag Hill, he enjoys a lot of local support. However, although having an impressive pedigree including MA Oxon and PhD Cantab, there has always been a question mark over his soundness. His earnest desire to embrace all views does offer some prospect of unreliability.

And that completes the field except for The Novice, the other local runner. At 50–1 he must be considered a rank outsider, but as Peter said, the race is open to all comers and that's one of its attractions. He looks steady enough, but we've never seen him run before. Back to Peter.

PETER: Thank you Julian. The runners are almost ready for the off, so here are the latest prices: The Bishop, now evens favourite; Mere Professor, at 3–1; Do Gooder, 10–1; The Rich Man, 16–1; and The Novice, 50–1.

(As the race begins, the runners run on the spot, moving slightly forward or backward as appropriate and falling, etc. when the time comes.)

And they're off, in the Millmead Pearly Gates Hurdles, over a mile and seven furlongs. And as they come up to the first hurdle, Basic Theology, it's The Bishop up by half a length on Mere Professor, then Do Gooder, and The Rich Man, and behind them The Novice. An easy flight this, The Bishop jumps cleanly perhaps a length up on Mere Professor now, Mere Professor two lengths up on Do Gooder, half a length away from The Rich Man, and then its The Novice. Going into the turn, it's The Bishop pulling away from Mere Professor as they run uphill to the next hurdle, Good Works. A long haul this and Do Gooder and The Rich Man are in their element up the hill, they're catching Mere Professor. The Bishop is over first, brushing the top of that one, losing a little ground; and behind him its Do Gooder who lands next, a beautiful jump, pulling away from Mere Professor and The Rich Man in the air; and after Do Gooder, its The Rich Man a head up on Mere Professor and then The Novice struggling to stay in touch. They're all over the second as they race away to the next jump, Church Attendance, the easiest.

As they come up to Church Attendance it looks as if Mere Professor has just edged up on The Rich Man into third. Over first its again The Bishop, now three or four lengths away from Do Gooder, then Mere Professor, The Rich Man, and six or eight lengths away, The Novice.

They're maintaining these positions now as they swing round into the back straight and the first of those awkward flights for which this course is famous, The Virgin Birth. The Bishop's class is showing now, he's six lengths away from Do Gooder on the stand side. Mere Professor making ground quickly on the far side will catch Do Gooder at this one, then it's The Rich Man and The Novice. The Bishop jumps – and he's fallen, the favourite has fallen at The Virgin Birth. The Bishop just couldn't accept that one. Well, that's a turn up for the books, The Bishop a faller at The Virgin Birth. Will that leave the race open for Mere Professor, or has Do Gooder got the stamina to hold on?

The rest of the field are over safely and as they move on to the fifth hurdle, The Resurrection, it's Mere Professor taking up the running. Behind Mere Professor, The Rich Man has finally found his form, moving strongly past Do Gooder on the stand side; and behind Do Gooder it's The Novice. Over The Resurrection, it's Mere Professor, touching down only just ahead of The Rich Man, then Do Gooder and behind Do Gooder it's The Novice. They're in the same order as they come to the third last, The Needle's Eye. As they go into The Needle's Eye, Mere Professor and The Rich Man are neck and neck. Mere Professor has landed awkwardly, but The Rich Man is stuck. It's a difficult jump that one, The Rich Man was just carrying too much weight and he couldn't get through. He's still struggling to free himself, but Do Gooder is over and catching up Mere Professor, and so too is The Novice.

So, with two flights to go in this Millmead Pearly Gates Hurdles, it's Mere Professor from Do Gooder, and Do Gooder's catching Mere Professor as they come round the turn to the second last, and behind them comes The Novice. And Mere Professor is certainly tiring. He's been caught by Do Gooder. As they come up to the water, Sinner's Confession, it's Do Gooder from Mere Professor — only these two in it now and some lengths behind them, The Novice. And Do Gooder's stopped! She's refused at the water. Do Gooder has refused at the Sinner's Confession. Mere Professor is over. Do Gooder is going round for a second attempt — no she's refused again. Do Gooder just won't make the Sinner's Confession.

So, with only one flight to go, The Only Way, there's only really one runner in it. Mere Professor looks as if he's going to come in for one of the most remarkable successes of his career. As they come to the last, it's Mere Professor now fifteen to twenty lengths up on The Novice. But it looks as if The Novice is catching Mere Professor. I think Mere Professor is pulling up. He is. Mere Professor is pulling up at the last. No he isn't. He isn't pulling up, he's changing direction. He's gone over the rails. Well, Julian said there was some possible unreliability, but I didn't expect this. He had the race won, but he just wouldn't follow the course.

Well, that leaves The Novice. He's over the last. It doesn't look as if there's much left in him, but he's going to make it. He's made it and so the winner of today's Millmead Pearly Gates Hurdles is the rank outsider, The Novice.

Ralph Dickerson
© 1993 Millmead Centre

TICKET TO HEAVEN

Teaching Point: Only one way to God/Heaven
Characters: Gilbert, Ticket Collector, Ernie and Mum's voice.
Props: Tickets and Book of Life

TC: Hold it there young man. Just where do we think we're going?

G: Well, I don't know about you mate but I'm going in there.

TC: Well that depends.

G: Depends on what?

TC: Depends on your credentials.

G: Oh, I've got those. I took out an insurance policy with them in case I got burgled.

TC: I said CREDENTIALS, not Prudentials. I'm not talking about that type of insurance.

G: Oh. What are credentials then?

TC: It's something that tells me it's OK to let you go through the gate.

G: What is this gate anyway? Where am I?

TC: This is the Gate of Heaven.

G: Heaven? But how come I'm here? I thought you had to be dead to get here!

TC: That's right. You do.

G: But I'm not dead.

TC: You must be to be here.

G: But I don't FEEL dead. When you're dead, well . . . there's . . . nothing.

TC: Oh, a lot of people think that sir. The number of people that come here saying the same thing. But as you can see, there's more to life than living!

G: Well, now I'm here I'll just go on in. Fancy that! Heaven! *(Attempts to enter.)*

TC: Hang on. There's the matter of your credentials remember. Can I have your ticket?

G: Ticket? *(Finds a ticket.)* Oh yes, look.

TC: This ticket says, 'Gilbert has safely passed his cycling proficiency test.' I'm sorry sir, but this one won't do.

G: No! *(Finding another ticket.)* Well, try this one. This one's a good one.

TC: *(Reads)* 'Gilbert has passed his Boy Scout Good Neighbour test, showing outstanding ability in minding his neighbour's business!'

G: There, I told you it was a good one. Well, I'll get straight in now. *(Makes another attempt to enter.)*

TC: Not so fast. I'm afraid good works are not enough.

G: What about my Sunday School attendance card then? *(Produces card.)*

TC: 'Gilbert has never managed to miss a Sunday School outing yet.' Sorry, going to church isn't enough either.

G: I know. I've got it! My Blue Peter badge! You can get in anywhere with this, and for nothing too!

TC: Not even a Blue Peter badge will get you in here, I'm afraid. Excuse me please, there's someone else coming through.

(Ernie comes in, hands ticket to collector, gets the all clear and goes on through.)

G: How come he got in so easily?

TC: He had the right ticket.

G: Well, what does his say?

TC: It says, 'This person is entitled to enter God's Kingdom because he believes Jesus is God's son. He believes that he has done lots of wrong things that need to be put right, and that Jesus died to take his punishment for these. He has asked Jesus to share his life and has tried to obey everything God said.'

G: Cor! I've not got one of those.

TC: Well that's the only way you'll get in, I'm afraid.

G: Where can I get hold of one?

TC: You can't get them here. You have to get them while you're still alive.

G: Look, I'll just pop back and get one.

TC: You can't go back. It's too late now, you only get one chance at living.

G: Let me buy one.

TC: I'm sorry, you can't buy these. Anyway you haven't any money. You left all that behind.

G: But . . . I know, look in your book. They said in Sunday School that there was a book in Heaven with names in it.

TC: Oh, you mean the Book of Life. Well I could try I suppose. You might be a last-minute entry. What name was it?

G: Gilbert.

TC: Gilbert what?

G: Gilbert Ape.

TC: *(Looks down list.)* Ape . . . Gilbert . . . No sorry, no Gilbert Ape in here I'm afraid.

G: But where can I go? I can't go back you said.

TC: No, I'm afraid you can't, you'll have to go where everyone else goes when they don't have the right credentials. *(Points away from Heaven.)* That way! If only you'd thought about it while there was still time.

(Exit Ticket Collector towards Heaven leaving Gilbert alone and shocked. Pause.)

M: *(Offstage)* Come on Gilbert, wake up. You'll be late for school.

G: Oh, thank goodness it was only a dream. I'm still alive. I've got time to get the right ticket!

© Powerpack

NO OTHER WAY

It seems that I have all I need —
Home and friends to comfort me.
Why do I just feel sometimes I'm so alone?
Outwardly I might be faking
But deep inside my heart's been aching.
I don't know which way that I should turn.

Oh then you showed me there is no other way
You showed me a bright and brand new day.
You gave me a new direction,
Your great love won my affection.
You showed me the only way.

I followed gods of my creation —
Money, glamour, cheap sensations —
Searching for a meaning that my gods exist.
Working, eating, sleeping, playing,
A quiet voice seemed to be saying,
'Could be so much more to life than this.'

Oh then you showed me there is no other way
You showed me a bright and brand new day.
You gave me a new direction,
Your great love won my affection.
You showed me the only way.

No other way
No other way

Many people try to tell me,
New religions try to sell me.
Just what can I do to help my soul be saved?
One man dared to make a claim.
He said, 'Knock me down and I'll rise again.'
Only one man ever came back from the grave.

And now you show me there is no other way
You show me a bright and brand new day.
You gave me a new direction,
Your great love won my affection.
You show me the only way.

No other way
No other way
No other way
Now I believe in Him
I believe in Him
I believe

© 1993 Babs and Dave Hyde

YES! Jesus REALLY is the Only Way to God

So what's my next step?

The following prayer may be helpful:

Lord Jesus Christ,
I know I have sinned against you in my thoughts, words and actions.
There are so many good things I haven't done.
Please forgive me.
I am sorry for my sins and turn from everything I know to be wrong.
You gave your life upon the cross for me.
Now I give my life back to you gratefully.
I ask you to come into my life.
Come in as my Saviour to rescue me.
Come in as my Lord to control me.
Come in as my friend to be with me.
Thank you for hearing and answering me.
Amen.

'If anyone hears my voice and opens the door, *I will come in*.'
(Revelation 3:20)

In summary then, we have established that Jesus is the only way:

1 Jesus said that He is the only way
   'I am the way and the truth and the life. No one comes to the Father except through me.'
   (John 14:6)

2 Therefore, it is impossible for all religions to lead to God
   Hinduism believes in many gods; Islam (Muslims) insists that there is one; and Buddhism is non-committal about whether God exists at all.

3 He is the only way to the Father
   Jesus Christ reveals God to us as a Father. This speaks of His love, comfort, direction and discipline of us.

But why is He the only way?

1 Because of His unique birth
Jesus' birth was through the Holy Spirit (Luke 1:35). He had God as His Father and Mary as His mother. He was both divine and human.

2 Because of His unique life
He said, 'Do you want to know what God is like? If you have seen me you have seen God'. (John 14:8-11)

He said, 'I have the authority to forgive sins.' (Mark 2:10)

3 Because of His unique death
All men will have to die, but His death had great significance. When Jesus was on the cross He cried out, 'It is finished!' This word really means accomplished. All that He had come to do, notably taking away the sin of the world, was now completed.

4 Because of His unique resurrection
No one else has come back from the dead and remained alive for ever. Jesus predicted that He would before He died, but the disciples were unbelieving. Christianity only has a continuing relevance because its Founder is still alive.

So, what do I have to do?

Jesus said that there were two responses required:

1 Repent
This means that we turn AROUND from walking away from God, and turn AWAY from all the actions and attitudes we know to be wrong. At its heart it means to change. As we confess our need of Him God will work in us to bring about these changes.

2 Believe
Believe in Jesus Christ. Believe that He died for your sins on the cross.

Believe that if you invite Him He will come into your life.

Not only believe the facts, but also trust yourself to Him and commit your life to Him.

NOTES

Introduction

1 Jim Montgomery, *Dawn 2000: 7 Million Churches to Go*, Highland Books, 1990).

Chapter one

1 *1991 National Census* (London: HMSO, 1992).
2 MARC Europe Report for Surrey and its Districts, *Good News In Guildford*, 1992. Available from Chris Hildyard, 105 Wodeland Avenue, Guildford, Surrey GU2 5LD.
3 St Helens Council of Churches, *Youth – The Spoiling Harvest.*
4 MARC Europe Report for Surrey and its Districts, ibid.
5 Martin Robinson and Stuart Christine, *Planting Tomorrow's Churches Today* (Eastbourne: Monarch Publications, 1992).
6 Roger Ellis and Roger Mitchell, *Radical Church Planting* (Cambridge: Crossway Books, 1992).

Chapter two

1 Charlie Cleverly, *Church Planting – Our Future Hope* (London: Scripture Union, 1991), p.xx.
2 Mike Hearn, 'Planting People, the Human Factor', *Planting Papers*, No. 3 (Winter 1991).

Chapter three

1 *Journey Into Life* (Sunrise Video, PO Box 814, Worthing, West Sussex BN11 1TS). Based on the *Journey Into Life* booklet by Norman Warren.
2 *Kensington Temple's Manual for Church Planters* (London).

Chapter four

1 John Dawson, *Taking Our Cities for God* (Milton Keynes: Word, 1991).
2 *Good News Down the Street* (CPAS).
3 Martin Robinson, *A World Apart – Creating a Church for the Unchurched* (Eastbourne: Monarch, 1992).
4 Steve Chalke, *Good Question* (London: Scripture Union Sound & Vision Unit, 1992).

Chapter five

1 David Newton, 'Why No Superchurches?', Church Growth Digest (Autumn 1988).
2 David Shenk and Ervin Stutzman, *Creating Communities for the Kingdom* (Ontario: Herald Press).

Chapter six

1 John Finney, *Finding Faith Today – How Does it Happen?* (Swindon: Bible Society, 1992).

Chapter seven

1 David Goodyear, 'One Plus One = One: Establishing a Two-Congregation Church', *Church Growth Digest* Vol. 12, No. 2.
2 These notes were compiled for a Baptist Union consultation paper on church planting and have not been published.
3 This figure is an amended version of one used by David Goodyear in 'One Plus One = One: Establishing a Two-Congregation Church'.
4 Ibid.

Chapter nine

1 These graphs form part of the Guildford Church Census (March 1993) which was collated by Pete Brayne, leader of Guildford Community Church. Details from Pete Brayne, 14/15 Queen's Road, Guildford GU1 4JJ.
2 Peter Brierley, *Act on the Facts* (London: MARC Europe, 1992).
3 These are part of a larger survey, the final results of which can be obtained from Vic Robertson, Millmead Centre, Buryfields, Guildford GU2 5AZ.